CHRIST-CENTERED
CONSCIOUSNESS

John T. Ryan IV

BALBOA.
PRESS

A DIVISION OF HAY HOUSE

Balboa Press books may be ordered through booksellers or by contacting:

Balboa Press
A Division of Hay House
1663 Liberty Drive
Bloomington, IN 47403
www.balboapress.com
1-(877) 407-4847

Because of the dynamic nature of the Internet, any web addresses or links contained in this book may have changed since publication and may no longer be valid. The views expressed in this work are solely those of the author and do not necessarily reflect the views of the publisher, and the publisher hereby disclaims any responsibility for them.

The author of this book does not dispense medical advice or prescribe the use of any technique as a form of treatment for physical, emotional, or medical problems without the advice of a physician, either directly or indirectly. The intent of the author is only to offer information of a general nature to help you in your quest for emotional and spiritual well-being. In the event you use any of the information in this book for yourself, which is your constitutional right, the author and the publisher assume no responsibility for your actions.

Any people depicted in stock imagery provided by Thinkstock are models, and such images are being used for illustrative purposes only. Certain stock imagery © Thinkstock.

ISBN: 978-1-4525-7627-5 (sc)
ISBN: 978-1-4525-7629-9 (hc)
ISBN: 978-1-4525-7628-2 (e)

Library of Congress Control Number: 2013910703

Printed in the United States of America.

Balboa Press rev. date: 08/05/2013

Table of Contents

INTRODUCTION

This book is about a practical way to connect to Christ's truth within consciousness. By consciousness, I mean thoughts and feelings. Thoughts and feelings lead to actions, which is how one lives one's life. In every moment of life, one experiences thoughts and feelings. These all constitute a life. But how can one negotiate one's own consciousness and draw nearer to Christ unless he or she knows the truth about how to experience him? How can one draw nearer to Christ unless he or she knows how to negotiate the enemy? Indeed, all of this exists within one's consciousness in moment-by-moment thinking and feeling.

What if true joy and happiness is influenced by moment-by-moment choices in one's own consciousness? What if human consciousness is nothing more than an interaction between Christ and Satan? What makes up human consciousness? In my opinion, it consists of five things: thoughts, feelings, actions, conscience, and the will. These constitute a human consciousness.

What if "talking" to God was possible? What if it were possible to build a connection with God in one's consciousness? In my experience, God will begin to heal me right where I am in my own consciousness. He has already been there for longer than I can imagine. There is one force in my consciousness whose agenda is for me to spend eternity in heaven and another whose agenda is the opposite. They both exist in my own consciousness.

What if God's love is deeper and more beautiful than I could possibly imagine? What if I am not separate from it? What if all I have to do is learn how to connect to it and follow its lead? What if his love is powerful enough to heal anything in my life, as long as I am willing to work for it? What if God wants to change my consciousness from the inside out? What if God wants to teach me that society's ideas about happiness are wrong? What if God had a way to direct a person perfectly if he or she would only follow his or her conscience? What if the way God communicates with us was through our emotions and feelings? What if all you had to do was learn how to trust these?

What if communicating with God was as simple as learning to read one's thoughts and feelings? What if determining God's will was as simple as reading one's conscience? What if acting according to one's conscience was the doorway to happiness in this life and the next? What if the key to happiness was aligning my conscience with my will? What if the only way to be happy in this life and in the next is to apply the teachings of Christ in my own consciousness?

My goal in writing this book is to describe exactly what happened to me, the healing that occurred, and how to experience a direct relationship with Jesus Christ, one that can be felt moment by moment. Indeed, such relationship is possible. It is not without work. Essentially this book is a guide on how to form a deeply intimate, moment-by-moment relationship with Christ. I know such a relationship is possible.

The bottom line is that I can connect to Christ from wherever I am and begin to form a relationship. The spirit of Christ exists within my very own consciousness. What needs to be understood more clearly is exactly what human consciousness is. It is the interplay between Satan and Jesus Christ. I am not alone in my consciousness. I need to learn how to read it and discern the source of thoughts and feelings.

The beauty of this process is that it isn't intellectual. Anyone can do it. Christ cares that much about everybody, as long as they're willing to try to love him. God's Spirit is unmistakable. But then again, who teaches us how to negotiate our own consciousness? I am just a tiny spirit in a battle of much larger forces. I can feel this if I really pay close attention to it. This interaction between Christ and Satan is within me. I am getting closer to Christ or to Satan with each thought, feeling, and action. I must learn to pay attention to my movements of spirit. Consciousness is the constant interplay of these spirits. That is why some thoughts and feelings need to be constantly embraced and others constantly rejected.

One thing I want to emphasize is that I never would've gotten anywhere in learning these spiritual matters unless I was healed from repressed homosexuality by Christ. This was the centerpiece of my healing. My spirit was repressed at a very young age by Satan and needed deep healing. One of my intentions in writing this book is to expose Satan's goals. Through his oppression of my gay spirit, Satan tried to create a false self in which I lived for twenty-three years. This had everything to do with the oppression of the spirit of love. It was through the healing of my spirit that I began to learn so many things about myself and about the spiritual world in general.

Next I will discuss the important things for getting the most out of this book. First, a belief in God is essential. Specifically, it is important to believe in Jesus Christ as Lord and Savior. It is crucial to believe that anything is possible in Christ. It is also essential to believe that Christ wants us to live in a love-centered consciousness. This will take work, but it is essential in this process and in the spiritual life. Jesus wants to teach me everything that I will ever need to know. He will teach me in the most loving way I can possibly imagine. Now that the main points of this book have been discussed, it is important to discuss my story.

CHILDHOOD

—•—◄○►—•—

I was born prematurely on September 4, 1976. I grew up in a very loving Catholic household. I was not exceptionally spiritual as a child. When I was a little boy, I was fascinated with vacuum cleaners. (When I went to a new person's house, the first thing I did was ask to see their vacuum cleaner.) I also loved airplanes. I used to get my dad to take me out to the airport to watch them. I used to build model airplanes as well.

I know God was with me then. I remember going to church often as a kid, but I never realized how important it was to connect to the spirit of Jesus. What is very important is that I always did believe in God. My parents were very loving toward me, and I had everything I wanted growing up. God has always been good to me. The reality of God is amazing. I was a sensitive and gentle child, and this was a beautiful aspect of me.

I loved to play with Legos, especially building Lego airplanes. I also loved to have Beatrix Potter stories read to me. My favorite was *The Tale of Mr. Tod*. My father and I loved this story. I used to play "imaginary football" on a wall near my home with G. I. Joe action figures. I would entertain myself for hours doing this. One of my favorite TV shows as a kid was *The Incredible Hulk*. I used to pretend that I would turn into the Hulk when people made me angry. Mostly I was a gentle child. This suited my character and my nature.

If there is one thing I could change about my childhood, it would be my exposure to the belief that it was wrong to be gay. For as long as I can remember, I was taught that it was wrong to be gay. This was very damaging to my little soul. I remember that the number one way for one boy to insult another boy was to call him a faggot. Naturally it was difficult for me to start to accept my feelings about other boys when I started to experience these feelings at twelve years old.

I remember trying to drive all the feelings out of my consciousness, out of my body. I remember feeling ashamed and petrified of them. I just wanted to drive all the feelings away, and I thought that's what I had to do. I remember feeling deep shame and guilt about them. By agreeing with the shame instead of accepting my feelings, I made a deal with Satan. It was at this point in my life that Satan began to influence my consciousness. The truth is that I was being viciously attacked by Satan. Satan was the source of all the repression in me. Satan made me afraid of all my feelings.

Though I had no sexual feelings toward girls, I was so repressed that I convinced myself I wasn't gay. Estrangement from my heart was the primary wound. By running away from my feelings, I became centered in a false self. I learned to hate my sexual feelings at a very young age. I was never able to explore my sexual feelings at all. Looking back on it, I was taught to hate love. But the thing is that I'd never been taught to identify my gay feelings with Christ. It never occurred to me that Christ might be the source of my sexuality.

I never associated any of my thoughts and feelings with God or Satan. I thought my consciousness was separate from both and that I was the source of all my thoughts and feelings. It was this assumption that allowed Satan to constantly trick me. This was true even though I believed in Satan's existence. My evil was the repression of my sexuality. I had a beautiful, gay sexuality and didn't realize it. But after the initial repression, I have very little remembrance of these feelings coming to the surface.

I tried to change my feelings to suit what I had been taught. I should've accepted my feelings as being good, regardless of what people thought. Instead, I believed it was wrong to be attracted to men and repressed my feelings. I had everything backward. It was Christ who gave me these feelings, but I didn't know that then. I never saw any of my thoughts and feelings as having an external source. I wish I'd had the courage back then to face being teased for being gay. But back then I kept thinking about the word *faggot*. I didn't want to be called that, and sadly, I didn't want to be gay. I didn't know any better.

I was also lacking in humility, but the world doesn't teach you to be humble. The world teaches that it's all about you. It teaches you that life is about being important. I believed everything the world taught me, especially about what it was to be a man. Deep down I didn't feel that way, and in Christ's eyes, there is nothing wrong with that. The result of all my mistakes was a very ego-driven personality. I was full of ego desire. I had the desire for an attractive girlfriend and worldly success. In my little mind, these were the only things that mattered. My feelings didn't fit society's definition of manliness. In hindsight there was nothing wrong with me, but I didn't know that then. The unfortunate thing is that our culture simply does not value gay maleness, but the truth is that it's a beautiful expression of God's diversity. At the time, I was completely in the grip of evil.

Notre Dame

In April 1995 I achieved a longtime dream of getting into the University of Notre Dame. One of the proudest moments of my life was telling my grandparents I had been accepted, because they loved Notre Dame. This was a new start in my life. I was not very popular in high school and had not enjoyed it much. Notre Dame gave me a chance to start over. At Notre Dame I began to experience more popularity. I found a crowd I fit into, and I had better luck with girls. I was popular for the first time in my life. I really thought my life was turning around for the better. I still had no sense of spirituality. I believed in Jesus Christ, but that was about it. There was no relationship.

Overall, Notre Dame is a very spiritual place, but I didn't take advantage of it. That's a shame because Christian spirituality is a beautiful thing. Like most college students, I partied on the weekends. This often included alcohol, which I used to deal with social anxiety, especially with girls. I still thought I was straight, so I was nervous around girls and needed something to relieve my anxiety. I could talk to them when I was drunk. However, my sexual experiences with girls always seemed to be missing something. My body just didn't respond. I thought it was because I was nervous. At the time, I didn't consider that I might be gay.

In my sophomore year, I started dating a girl named Hillary. She was two years younger than me and still in high school. She was very pretty, and I thought she was a good person. After we'd been dating for a while, I started anticipating having sex with her because this is what I thought was expected in a relationship. However, I continued to experience a lack of sexual arousal with her. I had no more excuses. I liked her and was comfortable with her. I wasn't worried about her judging me.

It was then that it became clear that I might be gay. I began to realize I had sexual feelings about men. At the time, this horrified me. I also deeply sensed that it was something I could not change. It became clear that I could not force sexual feelings with women—I just didn't have any. It didn't matter how badly I wanted to change this. At the time, it was painful. I thought it was my fault. It never occurred to me that God might be in control. Of course, God is in control of everything. It never occurred to me that sometimes God gives a person feelings that he or she can't change.

I began to feel inferior to other men. I also grew depressed and experienced a deepening self-hatred. I never realized I'd been living in self-hatred since puberty or that my negative thoughts were satanic in nature. That's how evil Satan is and how easily he's able to hide. I thought my feelings about being gay represented the truth about homosexuality, that I was inferior. This was the result of the messages of hate I'd received as a child. I couldn't talk to anybody about it. I was too ashamed. I had always thought people chose to be gay. Now I was getting my first glimpse of the truth: being gay is not a choice. God chooses your sexual orientation. That is a beautiful thing.

The idea that it was wrong to be gay was an evil deception. I never thought once I could turn to God at a time like this, but that was exactly what I should have done. It never occurred to me that this might be God's plan for me. It was just impossible to feel aroused by women.

Each time I was with Hillary after that, I tried harder and harder to be aroused. I felt like I was watching myself when I was with her. It was a horrifying experience. I can see now it was Satan torturing me. I sensed I would never be aroused by women. Only thoughts of men aroused me. I wanted desperately to change things. I felt totally alone, trapped in my own body, feeling things I didn't want to feel and thinking things I didn't want to think. I told nobody about it.

Being alone was the worst part. I never knew I had God with me all the time and that he loved me. I was not interested in a relationship with God at that point, and this was very sad.

I never allowed myself to experiment with my sexuality. I never allowed myself to fantasize about men. I just considered my gay desires to be the enemy. I was totally locked in a false self. I just couldn't admit to being gay. I hated myself more and more, wishing things were different. I thought acceptance of my homosexuality was not the solution to the problem but was the problem itself.

Thoughts of Jesus and homosexuality just didn't coincide in my mind. I had never conceptually combined the two, which was my biggest mistake. The comfort God could've provided in those days would have been exceptional, but I wasn't interested. Worst of all, I believed the world in so many ways, about everything it taught me about how to "be a man," and that just wasn't me. I was an effeminate spirit in a male body. I had all my self-value based on worldly ideas, and when my definition of masculinity collapsed, I had nothing left to fall back on. Again, I could have never imagined how much Jesus cared. All I knew was that my ego was crushed. I thought I was my ego, but later this proved to be a colossal lie. A relationship with God would've made all the difference.

I valued everything in the wrong way. Everything I thought held value in an ego sense held no value in Christ's eyes. That's why my desire to be straight held no power. That is why, despite the wishes of my false self, I could not change my feelings. Christ was always in control of my feelings, but I didn't know that yet. The worldly identity of my false self was falling apart before my very eyes, yet I tried to hang on to it. Because it was false, it held no power for stopping the truth. This was the truth I'd been trying to stop since I was twelve—that I was sexually attracted to men. I could not see this as beautiful. It felt anything but beautiful.

The effects of this awareness on my life were palpable. My grades began to suffer because I cared less about my life in general. I lost all the confidence that I gained in myself since high school. I didn't feel there was anybody I could talk to about my situation. I was afraid to admit to anybody that I might be gay. I didn't want to admit to anybody that I was struggling with my sexuality. I eventually broke up with Hillary. It was torturous being in a relationship with a female. I just had no feelings for her.

Drugs and Denial

It took me eight years after Hillary to admit to myself I was gay. Lying like this was an incredibly spiritual burden to maintain. I hated myself and my feelings. I was living in a totally false self, separated from God.

My discomfort with my body at this stage in my life was beyond words. I never let my body feel good sexually. I never let myself think about men, or what it would be like to be with a man. I was bound and determined not to be gay, to keep fighting it with everything I had. I thought I was inferior and wrong. My ego just could not take it, and this was the source of my true spiritual illness. I began to self-medicate my spiritual illness with drugs and alcohol. This is how I sought escape from my own consciousness.

Drugs and alcohol became a way to numb myself to all the turmoil in my spirit. In hindsight it's easy to see that this is the truth. At the time, I never knew my problems were spiritual. I would never have suspected that my real problem was separation from God. I never realized deep intimacy was possible with God. I hated myself and my body. I wanted to escape my feelings. Drugs became a dysfunctional way to do that. I began to smoke pot on a regular basis right after college. The only time the turmoil in my head would stop was when I was stoned. But all the drugs did was offer a temporary solution. As soon as they wore off, my problems returned. So I would get stoned again. This was a terrible abuse of my entire being, a self-torture through self-medicating. I used to escape my thoughts about what I felt in my body. I would never have suspected Satan was torturing me in those days, given the depression and anxiety I felt. I just had no peace and didn't know why, and drugs seemed like the only solution. All my drug use did was compound my spiritual problems. I suspect many people use drugs and alcohol because of these types of problems.

ACCEPTANCE

———•❖◄○►❖•———

In 2005, after seventeen years of fighting my sexuality, I was finally able to admit to myself I was gay. I finally decided to stop fighting my feelings. While I still didn't have any emotionally deep feelings toward men, I was able to feel enough sexually to finally accept my gayness. I finally allowed myself to think about men sexually. I realized I had to honor my body's feelings. I still didn't realize the whole of me was being repressed by Satan.

Still, being honest with myself didn't solve my emotional problems the way I thought it would. I still considered myself a "masculine man" even though I was gay. I was not in touch with my effeminate side. I didn't realize I was still living in a false self. In fact, I almost took pride in being more masculine than most of the gay men I knew. I had still not accepted myself. I still hated myself to the depths of my soul.

My spiritual problems (diagnosed as mental problems) persisted for the next six years. I continued to suffer from depression and anxiety. Even though I admitted to myself I was gay, I didn't see myself as effeminate. I was tricked by Satan. I didn't even realize that living in a false self was possible. It never occurred to me that that might be why there was very little joy or peace in my life. In 2011 I had a final mental collapse after at least three trips to the hospital for depression. The reason that my prior hospitalizations didn't work is that I was receiving psychosomatic treatment for spiritual problems. I had never accepted my real self. I was struggling with my feelings and thoughts and had never accepted Christ into my life. That is why my depression persisted despite medications—because I was living a false self. I believe the spiritual soul is at the root of many seemingly psychological problems, and this certainly was my case. Unfortunately, society is still too secular to admit this, but it's the truth.

Shortly after my final hospitalization, I began to see things that forever altered my life. Even after leaving the hospital for the final time, I still felt horrible. I never felt like doing anything. I had suicidal thoughts. The combination of never feeling like doing anything and having suicidal thoughts made me realize there was something very evil going on.

This was the first time I began to look at my consciousness from a spiritual angle. Satan has a knack for giving himself away. He is self-defeating. So for the time being, I kept following my thoughts and feelings, doing nothing. This made me feel worse. I never suspected Satan might be trying to control me. Life might not be about acting on your feelings all the time.

After feeling this way for a few weeks, one night I had an experience that forever changed my life. I had a string of negative thoughts and realized their source was something external from myself. I realized it was Satan. Until that moment, I had always thought my thoughts and feelings were my own. I just could not figure out why I felt so terrible all the time. I thought all my horrible feelings and thoughts were my fault. I never realized Satan could literally inject thoughts right into my consciousness. I always thought these feelings represented the truth of my consciousness. I saw that my thoughts and feelings now had an external source.

In some ways, this was most empowering experience of my life: I saw that I couldn't afford to identify with all my thoughts and feelings. I saw that Satan can be the source of thoughts, feelings, and perceptions. The enemy was Satan. I had just never realized that Satan could hide in my own consciousness. This is the truth. It was hard to believe how deceptive he was, that he could literally pretend to be my own thoughts and feelings. This perception gave me an entirely new attitude toward my negative thoughts and feelings. I realized these feelings and thoughts had been Satan in disguise. This was deep evil. It became clear that most of my thoughts and feelings were coming from Satan. Now that the evils of Satan had been exposed, it then became extremely important to work with Christ to heal. Christ had a beautiful plan for that too.

THE SMILE

The kindest thing Christ ever did for me began in the summer of 2011. I first noticed this when driving my car back from Washington, DC, to Pittsburgh. I had just gone to a golf tournament with my best friend, Jake. I noticed that my mouth started moving into an involuntary smile when positive and loving thoughts entered my consciousness. I knew only God could do this. What other explanation could there be? What else had the power to move my lips into an involuntary smile? I realized God was coaching me through my thoughts and feelings.

This phenomenon has continued for the last year. I'm lucky enough to talk to God. God truly has all power. The combination of realizing that Satan was in my own consciousness, plus the smile phenomenon has led me through countless spiritual discoveries. It is truly amazing to be able to receive God's input on everything. The amount of comfort I gain from this is beyond words. I never realized how much God cared about everything in my consciousness. This led me to believe I was truly living a very blessed life. To experience how much God cared about each and every thought that I had and to have negative thoughts was not easy. I knew I was sick, spiritually sick. Soon I started to have spiritual experiences that would continue to heal me, but the experience of the involuntary smile was what started everything.

THE CROSS

Regardless of the smile, and the recognition of evil in my consciousness, I was still very sick on Christmas Day 2011. I spent the day in Bellingham, Washington. While in church I looked up at the cross behind the altar. The next thing I knew, I felt power, combined with a feeling of love, coming out of it. It was one of the most beautiful things I'd ever experienced, and I knew Jesus was trying to talk to me. While I had always believed in Jesus, it was my first spiritual experience with the cross. I felt without a shadow of a doubt that Jesus loved me. I felt his desire to heal me.

It was the most moving moment of my life. I knew my life was in his hands. I had a deep sense of being called to Jesus. Jesus's love is the most beautiful thing in the universe. I had the deep sense that some sort of miracle was taking place, even though I was still having negative thoughts and feelings. It's hard to put into words the amount of wonder I felt. Jesus has an unlimited ability to communicate with spirits, and I knew he was choosing to communicate with mine out of love. It made me feel very special.

At this point I realized Satan was still influencing my thoughts and feelings. Jesus was also coaching me, so the healing process has begun. I had to "follow the smile" moment by moment. Since there was so much negativity in my mind, I realized I needed another source of consciousness, and this was my heart. It became easier to defy the negative thoughts when getting approval from Jesus. This was where God's infinite patience became clear: he stuck by me through my stream of negative thoughts and feelings. I got the sense that I had to reverse all my thoughts and feelings that were not reflective of the virtues. So I started to reverse them as soon as I experienced them. This worked. This is when I began to experience what I would call "the resistance." As I tried to become more positive, I felt resistance to it. Sometimes this felt like a brick wall of hatred. The key was realizing it for what it was. It was Satan. In the past, when I experienced resistance, I would've simply stopped. Now I did the opposite. Negative thoughts in my consciousness became something to fight. Positive thoughts in my consciousness became something to expand.

I started questioning the source of all my negative thoughts. When I would do this, a bolt of negative energy would hit me. Then I started to realize that this energy was attacking me constantly. This energy took multiple forms, but most of the time it tried to get me to do the wrong thing. I realized all negative thoughts were from Satan. He was able to inject negative thoughts directly into my consciousness. While I l knew I could not block them all, I began to defy them. This was an important spiritual step. Now the task became to fight the negative energy at whatever cost. Bad moods became something to fight. They were rooted in Satan. They were not something to believe in or serve. I began to challenge them.

One of the ways in which Satan would manifest himself was making me not feel like doing real work. I got very lazy toward the end of my spiritual illness. Once I realized these feelings were coming from outside me, I became committed to reversing them. I felt the resistance of my consciousness in the form of uncomfortable feelings, but eventually my actions started to change. I had a sense

15

that acting on negative feelings was serving Satan, and I didn't want to do that. When I started to engage this battle, I began to see that I had been an entirely self-willed person. I had never realized that certain feelings and thoughts simply cannot be acted upon.

I saw that I should not act on most of my negative thoughts and feelings. This path was not easy. Jesus wanted to transform my habit of following my own thoughts and feelings and acting on self-will. Instead, I would now determine what was the right action and do it regardless of how I felt. I had to start being productive when I felt like being lazy. Slowly but surely I grew more productive, even when I didn't feel like it. I knew these feelings were attacks from Satan. It began to look more and more like I was living in a satanic possession. Soon this would be proven to be the truth.

I had been fighting negative thoughts and feelings for weeks. I was stuck in my head. Then the truth was revealed in a flash. I was walking back from the gym one day and saw that what I'd been identified with in an ego sense was actually Satan. This was universe shattering. Like the first time I detected Satan in my consciousness, this realization was key to my healing. Satan had tried to create a false self with which I had identified. So in effect, the ego-driven part of myself was a distortion of Satan. I saw that what I had been identified with as myself did not exist and that my consciousness had been almost completely influenced by Satan. This is as evil as it gets. To influence a false self, and then to have that person following it around like it's the truth is evil beyond words. That is the truth about Satan. This again affirmed that I had to find an alternate identity. Once again this was my heart—or more specifically, my indwelling Christ. My head was filled with a total lie I could no longer identify with. Yet because of the repression of my feelings, I'd identified with my "head self" for a long time. I had always thought I was doing all of my thinking, and now it appeared it had been Satan-influenced. This was quite the revelation, so I had to start identifying with what I felt in my heart, which wasn't much at this time, but there was no alternative.

As is I tried to identify myself with my heart, Satan kept trying to push me back into thought. This is when I knew for sure I was possessed. I saw this would require separating from everything I thought I knew.

At this point I was extremely lucky to continue to experience the smile. I fought my false consciousness and tried to identify with my heart. I learned I had to spend all my time loving Christ. As I became aware of this, I also realized I had very little love toward anything. I was profoundly separated from love, and it was my responsibility to do the work to heal this. Deep down I knew the connection with Jesus in my heart was the solution. I realized I needed to love Christ all day long but still couldn't feel any love through all the resistance.

When I identified with my heart for any period of time, it would eliminate some of my negative thoughts. I knew I had to keep doing this in order to be sane. Often I wouldn't feel like going into the resistance, but deep down I knew that was exactly what I needed to do. I wasn't used to doing things that I didn't feel like doing. But I knew it would lead to something good, and Jesus kept leading me. Suffering is the path to Christ.

THE GOODNESS OF
MY GAYNESS

—•—◄o►—•—

While I intellectually knew it wasn't wrong to be gay, I never felt it emotionally. This hurt me deeply. I thought I had already accepted myself, but I had not. I had no crushes on men and very little feeling in my body. Most sadly, I had never developed a sense of deep goodness about my homosexuality. There was no deep acceptance of my spirit.

Then one day out of nowhere, the image of two men being together came into my mind, followed by deep sense of goodness that came from Christ. This was new. When I experienced it, I smiled. This was a profound sign from Christ of the goodness of my homosexuality. I had never experienced anything like this before. Satan quickly tried to wash the sense out of my consciousness, but the experience was mine. All of a sudden my mind opened up to the fact that it might be deeply good to be gay.

It gave me an entirely new perspective on myself and my sexuality. I had never associated my sexuality with Jesus before, but now I knew there was a direct connection. Effectively, this changed my view about homosexuality forever. The truth is that Christ loves homosexuality. I realized that all the negative thoughts and feelings I'd ever had about being gay had come directly from Satan. I began to know in my heart that Jesus wanted my feelings about my sexuality to reflect his truth. While I couldn't yet feel love toward men, this was an important start. I began to sense that I had had a real self that was repressed by Satan, one that was thoroughly good in its homosexuality, and that this was the self that Christ wanted me to experience.

Now I could believe all my negative feelings about my sexuality were from Satan. I began to try to reverse these perceptions. I sensed Jesus wanted me to love everything about my homosexuality as he did, and I sensed that my real self was very beautiful. This is when I started to remember the feelings I'd had about myself when I was twelve. I got the sense that Satan had attempted to murder my soul. I had to love my gayness as Jesus did to more fully experience my real self. It was about this time I realized I was living a life that could help thousands of gay people. Christ had created me as an effeminate gay man, and while I knew that some people would dislike my real self, their eyes did not matter. Christ's eyes are the only eyes that matter.

Now I began to get the sense that I had two selves—a false one that was the distortion of Satan, and a more effeminate real self, which was in Christ. This self was the opposite of the consciousness in which I had been living. This false consciousness was indescribable evil. I'd been tricked into living an entirely false self. Shame that created this false self was from Satan. That's when I started to see that our lives are played out on a battlefield bigger than we can possibly imagine. It was then that I started to have a deeply spiritual feeling about my real self, knowing it was close to Christ. This is also when I started to see its goodness and innocence. More specifically, I started to see the attack it had withstood since I was twelve. A miracle was taking place. My false self had been a stream of hatred and lies.

Satan can manipulate a consciousness this way, but this only happens when you agree with his evil. I'd agreed with a lot of his attitudes toward my real self. But now the truth was beginning to set me free. I realized why Christ was helping me so much when I saw how my real self had never been able to live. This gave me a sense of Christ's amazing goodness, and sense that something amazing was happening. I had a tremendous sense of knowing nothing but was open to something extraordinarily beautiful in Christ. I knew I was being raised from the dead and had a sense that Jesus was still performing miracles. There was a sense of tremendous sadness for having missed my real self for so long but also a sense of tremendous gratitude for it being "raised from the dead." This motivated me to get more out of the possession that held me. Satan tried to murder me when I was twelve and repressed my beautiful gay soul for my whole life, without my even realizing what was going on. It took divine intervention to save me.

I often thought back to lying in bed when I was twelve, feeling gay sexual feelings pouring through me, and saying to myself that I couldn't afford to feel them. I saw that I had made a deal with Satan and that this is when the possession started. Instead of having the energy of Christ pouring through me, I had taken on Satan's energy. Satan was the source of all the hatred, and by distorting my real self, he had made me a vehicle of that hatred. I was not a creation of hatred the way I thought. I was a creation of love that been viciously attacked, covered up, and hidden from my own consciousness.

I finally realized my whole consciousness was a stream of hatred and lies, and I was separated from my real self. There were many symptoms of this separation. One was a lack of feeling love for almost everything. Another was a constant stream of negative thoughts. Most of my consciousness was centered in my head and not my heart. I lacked feelings toward men. I knew the part of being a healthy gay man was having crushes on men, but I couldn't feel them. The worst symptom of my false consciousness was my lack of love toward Christ in my heart. I knew this was wrong, given how wonderful Christ is. I tried to get myself to feel love toward him but couldn't, and I had thoughts of disrespect instead. Since these were so insane, I knew they were coming from Satan. Every time I tried to experience love for Christ, I experienced severe resistance. It felt like going up against a freight train of hate. The negative thoughts were coming frequently. It was then that I saw one thought after the next was trying to drag me away from my heart.

It's hard to express in words what it's like to experience a stream of hatred like this. It was just one evil thought after the next, all day long. I could tell Satan was desperate to keep me away from my heart and the love within. Since I had not loved anything, it was hard to believe love was there. Yet somehow I knew it had to be found. When I identified with my heart, I felt bolts of evil energy shoot into it. Everyone needs to experience something like this to know they are being constantly attacked by Satan. All I knew was that I brought more hatred upon myself when I identified with negative thoughts or feelings. There was a great sense of walking in darkness. Having Jesus with me made everything helpful. My hope was that he would not leave me despite my evil thoughts.

I just tried harder to love Jesus all day long and to identify with my heart. This wasn't easy, considering the resistance I felt. I knew I was possessed and lacking in love, but the work required to get out was really hard. I started to learn that this was how Satan worked: he constantly tried to distract me when I was on track and doing the right thing. Since I'd been in his possession for a long time, he made doing the right things seem very uncomfortable. This was designed so I'd stop. He made it tempting to turn back, but I knew I couldn't afford to do that. I had seen the truth, and it wasn't pretty.

So I kept trying hard to love while having almost no experience loving anything. This was one of the hardest parts of the process. At this point, my consciousness did not reflect the virtues. I was inundated with hateful feelings that I had to resist. But in doing so, I became willing to deny myself, which was really important in Christ's eyes.

It was in doing this work that I realized how powerless I was without Christ. It was amazing how quickly my consciousness would deteriorate when I got back into mental identification. By this I mean identification with ego thoughts. It was in this phase that I had to be absolutely willing to go into resistance and constantly love Christ. The temptation was to avoid the resistance. I couldn't take the bait because it made me feel worse. The solution was to love and to continue to go through it, and seeing the discomfort was a sign I was doing the right thing.

As I battled Satan and tried to move closer to love, I started to use thought reversal again. When I experienced a negative thought, I immediately reversed it and believed the opposite. There were so many times Satan tried to convince me I was going to have a bad day, and I immediately reversed that belief. Through this technique, many of my thoughts were proven to be lies. I had to do this all day, and it was a struggle. One thing I realized was that hatred didn't make sense. It didn't make sense to have trouble loving Christ all day long.

Jesus showed me at one point that my heart-consciousness was the beginning of the solution to my problems. The process was not easy. That was the point. Following Jesus is not easy, especially when it involves suffering to connect your heart. I had to go through the daily resistance for months in order to center my consciousness in my heart. Each time I focused on identifying myself in the area of my heart, I encountered an even fiercer stream of negative thoughts and feelings trying to distract me. This was where I learned something very important: Satan fights very hard when one is close to having a spiritual breakthrough. He just doesn't want you to get closer to Christ. I knew I needed a sense of self that was centered in my heart and in worship of Christ. The resistance was so fierce that I had trouble experiencing it. This seemed horribly insane. I was so deeply possessed that when trying to love Christ, I experienced extremely negative thoughts and feelings. I was ashamed of my inability to experience love for him. I knew this was inexcusable, given that he was trying to save me. I needed a breakthrough.

I knew my struggles with feeling love toward Jesus were insane. In hindsight Jesus knew I needed a special experience to solve this problem. Then one day I was driving, and I started to think about Christ. Suddenly I felt a surge of majesty, perfect love, and glimpses of eternal life. In the past I had had some experiences of Christ's love, but this was the most profound experience of him I'd ever had. It's hard to explain something this beautiful. It was the most majestic feeling I'd ever felt in my life. I felt how much he loved me, and I've never had a problem loving him since. He knew this was exactly what I needed, and after this experience I began a much more determined effort to love him. He is love, after all.

Gay Love Breakthrough

Not surprisingly, after being viciously attacked by Satan for months, I had a breakthrough in April 2012. I'd already sensed I was a deeply repressed homosexual. I also sensed that I needed to experience gay love but had never been able to feel anything close to that. I never had been able to love another man, even in my imagination. This was truly sad.

The sadness would be replaced by a miracle. Seemingly out of nowhere, after weeks of trying to experience love for Christ with no luck, I was able to imagine and feel love for another man. I felt that my capacity for this was real. This was huge. This proved it was possible. I now knew gay love did exist. It was like coming out of spiritual deadness to life. Christ was truly raising my spirit from the dead. What I had never been able to even experience before I was now feeling.

Being able to deeply feel my heart for the first time made all the difference. The message I'd gotten as a child was that heterosexual love was the only form of love. This lie had now been wiped out. It was like waking from a nightmare. Jesus was the source of this. Now Satan could not repress it from my consciousness anymore. I began to see why he'd been fighting so hard in the few months prior. Now I knew gay love did in fact exist. I cannot express what it meant to know I did have the capacity for gay love. It was truly sad that I had not experienced this in my life before. All I had known was hatred of homosexuality, even though it was my own.

This was like opening a new consciousness. It was the most beautiful thing about me, outside of my direct worship of Christ. This reinforced the truth that my sense of self had been totally false and that Christ loved my real self. I felt a deep sense of being healed. There was also a sense of wonder at gay sexuality, and the sense of having missed out on something beautiful. This is a truly a Christ-centered experience. Now Jesus was bringing it back into my awareness. There was immense new value in the effeminate male self that I was. There was a sense of radiant splendor in Christ. So now when I felt sexual feelings, I knew Christ was the source.

By hating my sexual feelings, I had hated Christ. This was the biggest mistake I'd ever made, but he forgave me. Hatred of love is insane. It is the most evil thing that you can teach a person. I now clearly saw that hatred of gay people is hatred of Christ. This was a stunning revelation. I saw my self-hatred from an entirely new angle. My beautiful gay self was in Christ. It's hard to put the beauty of this into words. I began to have a new relationship with my body and soul. I knew that any feelings of "less than abundant love" for my sexuality were from Satan.

. This revelation caused the malicious thoughts to lose their power. I began to experience a sense of deep intimacy with Jesus. I clearly saw how Satan had tricked me into hating my gay love. This goodness within me was amazing beyond words, as is everything associated with Christ. The ability to more fully experience my homosexuality was to be able to experience Christ directly.

I saw that nothing had been more evil than the hatred of my homosexuality. Each time I experienced my homosexuality in a deeper way and loved it, Jesus smiled at me. The experience of beginning to be happy and confident about something I had only experienced hate for previously was beyond words. This is the beauty of God. Jesus loves my effeminate gay self. Feelings of less than confidence were coming from Satan.

Now I experienced a sense of splendor associated with homosexuality, which was its truth. I felt the radiant love in my body, and my soul's acceptance of Christ. I clearly saw that the real evil had been in the rejection of my beautiful gay self. I felt that the goodness of my sexuality was beyond words. This was the goodness of Christ in me. There was a sense of tremendous evil in its repression. There was also a sense of Christ having been in control of these feelings all along, and rejoicing in their return to life.

I realized I was being raised from the spiritually dead. There was a deep sense of Jesus training my heart to love and an almost inexplicable sense of wonder at having been created this way. I felt an abiding sense of his presence and love. I was beautifully gay. Just to say that was a huge step. I started to feel my natural attractions toward other men. The truth began to shine in my consciousness. What I had been taught my whole life was not in Christ indeed was. Now I realized I needed to start acting according to my newfound feelings, and honestly, it was like going through puberty again at age thirty-five. I wondered how I'd been able to live so long without feeling these feelings. But that had been part of the battle between Christ and Satan.

Christ's truth was in everything I was taught that was not lovable. It was hard to put into words the value of a healthier gay self, a sense of real gayness being deeply in Christ. I knew I was experiencing something out of the realm of the ordinary. Christ was revealing to me the truth about homosexuality. What was beautiful beyond words was the sense of gay love being in the form of Christ's love, and part of its diversity. He deeply approved of it. I was taught by the world that gay love did not have much value. This belief had hurt me for years. Now I was getting my Creator's deep approval. I knew my homosexuality was Christ's love. I knew the two energies were not separate. My homosexuality began to look truly sacred.

A beautiful gay spirit is so loving and gentle that it is beyond words. Within me it had been deeply distorted. I believe every person has a real self who is formed in Christ. Our personal choices determine our connection with this spirit. When we make bad choices, we separate ourselves from it. To maintain our connection to it, we must suffer Satan's attacks. There is no avoidance of suffering. My beautiful gay spirit had suffered from Satan's evil for a long time.

I began to see that Satan had fooled me in many ways in terms of how to relate to other men. For most of my life, I saw other men as the competition. I associated them with everything other than love. I was just uptight around other men, and totally cut off from love. Then I began to think about holding hands with men, and loving activities with other men. It was then I started seeing more glimpses of the real me. I saw that I loved to hold hands with men.

This gave me a wonderful sense of how to relate to other men that I'd been lacking. This was how Christ made me, and to separate from everything else was wonderful. My sense of false masculinity had been a satanic trick. This had dominated my consciousness for more than twenty years. The feminine had been what I'd rejected because I didn't think a man should feel that way. But that's not what Christ thought. He made it clear to me by smiling me every time I embraced my feminine side. Soon this began to free my soul. I began to be deeply proud of this. This was beautiful, since I had rejected these feelings in myself for so many years.

EXPANDING SENSE OF CHRIST

Along with the expanding sense of goodness in my gayness, I also experienced an expanding sense of Christ. I started having spiritual encounters in which I experienced his radiant goodness. Many happened in church. One consisted of seeing an image of myself as a little baby followed by a tremendous feeling of love. I started experiencing this goodness soon after I embraced my beautiful gayness. There is clearly a connection between the source of love and its expression. These experiences always brought tears to my eyes. It is impossible not to be moved to tears when experiencing Christ's goodness. I believe anyone who ever experiences this will immediately identify with the truth of Christ. Christ's love is the most beautiful thing in the universe and the most beautiful thing a human being can ever experience.

I've had some specific experiences of Satan's hate. It's as hideous as it gets. There are no words to express how evil he is and the extent to which he will go in trying to push a soul away from Christ. Thank God he failed in my life. This takes constant work to keep up. Realizing that his evil is outside of you is the key. That's when the negative thoughts and feelings lose their power. Satan's hate feels like a deep, dark, and black rage. He is hatred for anything and everything. He makes no sense. What is truly hard to understand is why Satan hates in this way. How can one hate love? However, his only true power comes when you believe his lies.

The problem is that most people are not easily able to see Satan in their own thoughts and feelings. He hides easily. The truth is that in this life we are never free from his attacks. I believe so many people's problems come from Satan, and they don't even realize it. They don't realize they're being attacked by something external. They experience all their thoughts and feelings as their own and don't suspect that an outside source might be influencing them.

Satan wants us to think we are sovereign over our thoughts and feelings. He can then inject all kinds of negativity and have one blame oneself for it. Satan wants people to live in their sinful ways and never question them. Most importantly, he wants one never to realize he is attacking. This was my case. But I learned to pay really close attention to my spirit, especially to feelings of discouragement when I tried to do something right. The truth is that Satan was trying to attack me all the time, trying to ruin my spiritual life. The more I questioned the source of my negative thoughts and feelings, the more I noticed his evil energy.

The more I questioned the source of my evil thoughts and feelings, the more I felt his energy attacking me. As I did this, I realized more of the truth of my own consciousness. I realized it needed to be fought. Each day was a spiritual battlefield. For me, it was noticing that I didn't feel like doing the things I should do. Resistance to experiencing positive things was clearly from Satan. I realized if I did what I felt like doing all the time, I was serving him. Often this meant doing uncomfortable things. It was difficult to break the habits of always doing as I pleased, but that way of life was sinful.

Satan tries to make doing the right thing as difficult as possible. Resistance makes it harder to do the right thing. For me, the temptation was to avoid real work. I imagine this is tempting for a lot of people. Satan constantly induced feelings of not wanting to work. Then he would try to convince me that God would reward me for less than my best effort. This was a lie. I had to learn to resist this temptation. All avoiding work does is create more work. Sometimes I had to learn the hard way. If I wasn't here to work for Christ, why else would Satan create resistance to it? This was the crux of the problem. I had to learn to work hard again. The more resistance I felt to a particular task, the more I needed to do it. This meant making the difficult choice over and over again.

Each day Satan would try to make me avoid proper tasks. Each day I would have to choose to feel uncomfortable to get the task done and then would feel joy after completing it. This I learned was the centerpiece of the spiritual life. Doing what you feel like doing all the time is not the way God intended us to live. So I began to seek out the tasks that I didn't feel like doing. I knew the discipline and hard work would save me, as with my love of Christ.

IDENTIFICATION OF SATAN
IN MY CONSCIOUSNESS

—•—◄O►—•—

After becoming aware of the dangers of ego identification and the fact that Satan was masquerading as my own thoughts and feelings, I had to accept that Christ had all power over my consciousness. I had to identify the ways I was still trapped in sin. For me, sin was having an attitude of not wanting to work. I had the attitude of a spoiled child. Jesus wanted me to learn how to work for happiness in him. My resistance to real work was evil. I had to remember that I could not just identify with all my thoughts. I had to discern spirits. I knew Satan could sneak into the depths of my consciousness. I knew he must be defied and denied. I knew he was the temptation to be lazy. He was literally in my own consciousness. This is what I believe most people don't realize. Satan and Christ are literally in your own consciousness, with Satan representing everything that is evil and Christ representing everything that is good. We are tiny human beings in a big spiritual battlefield

While Satan could try to influence my thoughts and feelings, he could not control my actions. He could make it difficult to do the right thing, but in the end the choice was mine. The more I practiced doing good, the easier it became. This often involved making a difficult choice each day to do the right things in spite of my feelings. I learned laziness was not an option. I learned that choosing the lazy option would worsen my mood. Doing the right thing was not easy. I learned that taking a positive action would heal a mood. Once I began to practice this on a regular basis, I began to see how sovereign Jesus was over my feelings. Although I had to choose the difficult path on many occasions, taking the right actions always made me feel better. It was Jesus who blessed me with these feelings. He is in control of my spirit.

I started to see that doing the easy thing was often wrong. The quick fix was not the solution, it was the problem. Gaining eternal life is not supposed to be easy. This is the truth. Then I started to think about Jesus's instructions to deny self and take up one's cross. Taking up my cross was doing all the things I didn't feel like doing. Doing them with love was the only option. I began to see that love was work and work was love.

It was also revealed that doing what Jesus taught was the best predictor of a good mood. God has power over our moods, and our moods are always tied to our spiritual condition. I learned that when I would think properly, I encountered resistance that I could literally feel. Often this would feel like something I could not get through. Perseverance was the key. Satan is a liar and a coward. I had to learn to go into the resistance. Slowly but surely I began to have an easier time thinking and feeling with more love. It's a concerted effort to try to be a better person, and one must engage it moment by moment.

I realized that loving Jesus was a constant process, especially if I really wanted to be happy. He is in control of my spirit and allows me to suffer when I deviate from his path. That does not mean he stops loving me. Jesus is the only path to happiness. I learned that I had to think about him all the time if I wanted to improve my thoughts and feelings. This wasn't always easy. This resistance could be felt. Once

I realized it was Satan, I could go through it. I learned that if I truly thought about Jesus all the time, he would change my consciousness. But this resistance could be felt.

Loving Jesus strengthened his presence. This meant more joy, love, peace, and general fellowship with him. Loving Jesus meant the rejection of everything that was not virtuous. This was not easy. I learned I had to reject thoughts and feelings all day long. I felt two energies going back and forth within my own consciousness. It also took following my conscience all day long to help discern Jesus's will. Jesus can provide radiant joy, but I must do things his way and try to love him all day long. Again I cannot emphasize the importance of practicing this.

Whether I realized it or not, Jesus was in my thoughts and feelings, as was Satan. More importantly, Jesus was in my heart. I had a difficult time connecting through all the resistance. Satan did not want me to do this. Jesus can talk to me constantly through my heart. I learned that if something didn't resonate in my heart, it probably wasn't real. Everyone has a spiritual heart. Jesus uses it to communicate with us. I just had to learn to follow it. The ego mind can be disconnected from Jesus. The heart is not. While person may not experience a smile on his or her face like I do, one can experience feeling his or her heart and its responses to thoughts and actions. The ego self is Satan's domain and is full of deception. The spiritual heart is Jesus's realm.

I learned to pay attention to what was going on in my spiritual heart. I adjusted my thoughts and actions based on what I felt in my heart. I learned that I had to go through some very fierce resistance. It came in the form of distracting negative thoughts, negative feelings, and a sense of wanting to give up. The bottom line is that sometimes the ego mind is the enemy. The heart gives a much greater sense of what you are truly feeling. It just takes daily practice to get in touch with it. I had to realize that loving Jesus was something I had to do constantly.

I had to see that my ego was an evil deception. I believe that Jesus created me for fellowship with him in my heart. As long as I didn't believe everything my mind told me, I kept getting better. The smile would come just about every time I rejected the pompous ego self. This self was very self-hating. I had to replace its hateful thoughts with more humble ones. The false self was a satanic manipulation. Only the spiritual heart of my real self could be trusted. I began to experience more joy in Christ by ditching ego identification completely. There was always resistance. Thoughts kept trying to pull me back into my head. There was also a desire for more comfortable path to Christ, but I knew there wasn't one.

There were also thoughts of having false power. All I knew is that my ego self was a liar. These were not representative of my real self in Christ in any way. What I never understood prior to being saved by Jesus was how deeply Satan could influence my own consciousness. He got into my head and I didn't even realize it. I just thought all the negative thoughts and feelings were the truth. My whole life I was plagued by negative thoughts and feelings but never considered that they might be satanic. I was constantly serving Satan by believing them. What Satan really wanted was to fool me my entire life. I couldn't fight something when I thought I was the source of the problem. When it became clear that my enemy was Satan, things changed. I learned from Jesus and experienced great joy in rejecting my thoughts and feelings that were not reflective of the virtues, although that was uncomfortable at first. Even though it felt like I was fighting myself, I had to keep going into the smiles.

This was doing the right thing. I just could not act according to my thoughts and feelings all the time, or I was serving Satan. I learned that I had to make a choice. The choice was to serve Christ. I had to accept that level of responsibility in order to do good. If not taking an action was serving Satan, then I had to do that action with love, no matter how I initially felt.

The temptation to be lazy is how Satan manifested himself in my consciousness. He may manifest in different ways to different people. Whatever way, the agenda is the same. Satan wants to separate a person from the joy of following Christ. I found that reversing my thoughts worked frequently when tempted to do the wrong thing. I learned that I had to get out of my comfort zone. Changing behaviors is a form of carrying the cross, and it was not easy to do, yet it was much better than serving Satan.

Once I was able to determine that a lot of my feelings represented Satan's hate of my real self, I saw they were not true to me. This meant that I had to fight them. It constantly required doing the things that I didn't feel like and doing the right thing while engaging the discomfort. In this way I learned that culturally induced solutions to spiritual problems never work. Satan is a master of deception and will do anything to make you identify with his ways, rather than thoughts and feelings that are in Christ.

Since I was living in a false self, I learned it was critical to cease ego identification. I had to break identification with negative thoughts. I learned that when I believed lies, I experienced more of them. It was critical to remember that Satan is a liar. It robbed him of his power over my consciousness when I stopped believing his lies. When I stopped believing a negative thought, it disappeared from my consciousness. I had to resist as many negative thoughts as I could. This was the key to fighting Satan. It was in being willing to put in the work. Satan tried to make me avoid the resistance. Doing the right thing meant being uncomfortable. There is no comfortable way to build new habits.

Often when something felt like it was the last thing I wanted to do, that meant I needed to do it immediately. This was how Satan influenced my consciousness, and changing my ways was not easy. I learned that no matter what the action, I needed to maintain a positive attitude. Jesus will always reward hard work. The key was always using my conscience to determine the right action or thoughts. I also had to be willing to be attacked when doing good. This was absolutely the case in embracing my sexuality. Satan made me feel uncomfortable or negative as I embraced it, and the smiles from Christ were profound. Acceptance required going through resistance. The rewards of acceptance were so vast and the love so profound that it made me want to do it every time. I learned I had to go through resistance again and again.

As I learned to feel, I realized Christ was influencing every part of me that was good. My sexual feelings were part of that. My love for Christ was the only thing that was more important. Out of nowhere I started feeling attracted to men. It was like going through puberty at age thirty-five. I was able to see that my sexuality was the spirit of Christ in me. Rejecting it was the direct rejection of Christ. This was not a good idea. Jesus had been in control of my sexuality my entire life. He was bringing this deeply intimate part of me to life, and it was a beautiful process. I saw that I had had everything backward. Feelings I thought were the enemy were the creations of Christ himself. I had been directly hating Christ and not realizing it. This is as insane as it gets and is clearly in Satan's realm.

Shortly thereafter I began to experience my sexual feelings in terms of holiness. This was another huge step. Holiness was not something I had associated with my sexuality. This was the truth. Gay sexuality is holy when it's in the context of love. This transformation from seeing my feelings as bad to seeing them as holy is a testimony to the power of Christ. The truth about gay sexuality is that it is deeply in Christ. The awakening of my feelings made it clear that Christ knew my soul deeply in love, and this was no surprise. This gave him absolute authority over my feelings. As I became more accepting of them, I got increasingly tender smiles from Christ.

I knew this represented the truth about how Christ felt about my gayness. He thoroughly wanted me to love and enjoy it in all its dimensions, from romantic to sexual. I learned I could only feel these feelings by loving them deeply. It is truly wonderful to feel in love with my real self and everything it represents. Everything I was taught had no value by society had massive value in Christ's eyes. It was wonderful to see how much Christ approved of my real self, not the masculine-acting false self. I had to learn to completely disregard the false self. This required going through a massive amount of resistance. What do I really mean by "going through the resistance"? I encountered this when I shifted my thoughts and feelings to the virtues. Satan tried to cause thoughts and feelings according to his evil agenda. Going through the resistance meant going through feelings of discomfort in doing right. Satan wanted to block my change, to have me continue along the path of least resistance.

In my experience the path of least resistance brings no joy. When I do something the easy way, I feel worse. I may avoid some work, but the path of least resistance leads to misery. When faced with a choice between doing something the difficult or easy way, the difficult way often leads to satisfaction in the long run. Change takes discomfort, but it almost always pays off. Anytime a person tries to change, there will be resistance. Countless times I discovered that joy was the result of doing something difficult, and the times showed me that the initial resistance was Satan.

When I went through enough resistance, I started to make progress. Many times the resistance to changing my ways of thinking and feeling was from Satan. I had to work on my own consciousness. I was responsible for what I thought and felt, not an innocent victim. Christ is everything, and I must fight for the truth of what he taught. I learned that following any lies of consciousness made me miserable. I had to push through the resistance and follow the virtues no matter what. I could not afford to always think and believe those things that initially came into my consciousness. I learned I had a choice in how to respond to them. If something was not reflective of the virtues, it was probably from Satan.

I learned to use thought and feeling reversal. When I experienced a negative thought, I immediately reversed it to something more positive. Christ is everything that is representative of the virtues. I had to go through this process all day long. Because I didn't have the power to block out all negative thoughts, I had to work on reversing them. This involved a daily battle. My willingness to do the hard work was the difference. With it I was amazed at how quickly I could change my consciousness. My love for Christ was in constantly seeking goodness. While this didn't mean having to be perfect, it meant trying to shift my consciousness as much as possible. I had to be patient when I didn't feel like it. I had to love when I didn't feel like it. I had to work when I didn't feel like it. I was amazed at how much I could reshape my entire consciousness. However, I knew the power to do this wasn't mine, it was Christ's. Through working hard I found it easier to overpower my negative thoughts and feelings. The power truly was Christ's.

Through the use of the spiritual tools, it became clear there was little spiritual middle ground. I was either surrendering to Christ and participating in his joy, or I was in Satan's domain of evil. I learned that I made moment-by-moment choices. This was my way of serving Christ. It was either this or choosing a self-willed life. I learned that I needed to act my way into better thinking, not vice versa. In the past Satan tricked me into thinking I should only act according to how I felt, avoiding actions I didn't feel like taking. This was a truly evil way to live. I've learned that if I do the right thing, the good feelings come. Christ truly has power over my moods. My moods are dependent on my actions. When I take back self-will, I feel worse. Sin does not feel good. While the way of the virtues may feel more difficult at first, it always leads to a greater sense of peace and joy.

The point is that the way of the virtues will feel more difficult at first, especially when I am trying to escape Satan's grasp. It depends on how deeply I have embraced his evil ways. Evil is anything that goes against the virtues. Satan created a certain amount of discomfort in attempting the right thing. I had to deal with these feelings in order to progress in the spiritual life. There is no easy way to progress in the spiritual life. I could choose the easy way or the way that worked. Everything about the way of the cross worked, and the path of least resistance failed. There is a certain amount of suffering that is unavoidable when living the Christian life. To me it is the discomfort that one has to go through when they do the right thing on a regular basis. It is choosing to take the difficult path on a repeated basis. There is no avoidance of this kind of suffering.

I could live according to the virtues and learn to resist Satan's temptation to do the wrong thing, or suffer more. Satan is so deceptive that he tricks you into thinking that doing what you feel like doing will work. This is not true. Joy comes from doing what is right, not what is easy. Unfortunately, we live in a self-willed society in which virtue is not celebrated. In reality everything is under Christ's control. The only true joy is in serving Jesus, even though it's not easy at first. People cannot will themselves to joy. Joy has to come naturally from Christ.

Feeling My Heart for the First Time

The hardest part about spiritual discoveries was to immediately put what Christ revealed into practice. For more than twenty years, I had been disconnected from my heart. This was a horrible way to live. I was unable to feel love toward just about anything. I lived in a sad, depressed, and murderous consciousness. It was a living stream of hatred and lies. As Jesus healed me, I began to feel my spiritual heart, the beautiful gay heart that I lost for twenty-three years. It was more beautiful than I could've ever imagined. Right before I began to feel my heart, I went through heavy resistance. In trying to focus on my heart, I felt evil energy attacking it. I had to persevere through that in order to feel. When I was finally able to feel it, it was euphoric. I would imagine dating and felt my heart come alive with excitement and joy.

However, Satan kept calling me "faggot." I knew I had to go through this resistance. There was still some deep hatred covering up my beautiful heart. This led to another breakthrough, this time in being able to read my heart. I began to focus my consciousness on my heart and see what it was saying. This was very revealing because it showed that I was having negative reactions to God's love. Deep in my heart I was still angry at God for making me gay. In effect I was still being belligerent toward Jesus.

I set out to correct this and conversed with my heart in a way I hoped would please Jesus. I had to tell the energy that was covering my heart to stop being so belligerent. It was totally insane, and I could not believe I still felt rage over being gay. This rage was so deep in my soul that I couldn't see it previously. This is how badly Satan tried to hide the truth from me. This was the source of my false self. It's hard to put into words what fighting this type of evil is like, something that just wanted to kill my gentle gay soul. This is what Satan tried, and most people don't realize they are being attacked. After a while I got used to fighting him. I saw that my gentle gay self was winning. It was euphoric. Disciplining my angry heart was one of the final steps. It was hard to get my spiritual heart to be kind toward Jesus at first, and this was insane. I didn't even know that my heart was rebelling like this. It took months of work just to get to the point where I understood what it was saying and feeling. After finally taking care of this part of the process, I began to integrate my heart and head.

While I love feeling my gay feelings, I had to learn how to stop disrespecting myself. Disrespectful words in my consciousness would kill the feelings. Jesus had a remedy for the problem, an experience showing how deeply my spirit was attracted to other men. This was what Satan had been trying to crush. Jesus gave me a sense of infinite beauty in this spiritual truth. I felt the depth of attraction much more than before and knew homosexuality begins in the spirit. This was the deepest sense of approval I had ever gotten of my sexuality. There was a sense of eternal glory in it. Jesus showed me how deeply my spirit was attracted to other men and how beautiful it was. Somehow this experience wiped out the disrespectful words that permeated my consciousness. This led to a deeper experience of beautiful, gentle gayness. I felt the true beauty of my spirit. I experienced my sexuality from a different perspective. The healing was beyond words.

When I first realized Satan was in my consciousness as a stream of lies and negativity, I experienced nothing but this suppression of my homosexuality. As Jesus blessed me with more beautiful experiences of my gayness, I got the sense of Satan fleeing, through a reduction of negative thoughts. I had a deepening sense of love toward Jesus. My rebellion against my beautiful gay heart had started when I was twelve. Jesus forgave me and took me into his loving arms.

Being just a "little gay" wasn't good for enough for Jesus. He wanted me to be radiantly gay. I started to notice that I got an extra-special smile when I accepted this with all my heart. I experienced Jesus's ultimate power. It was wonderful to submit to his will. This always brings joy. As long as I was willing to submit to doing some work, it was all worth it. There's nothing more beautiful than Jesus's truth. Doing hard work causes Satan to flee. As he retreated, I had to find the resistance and stay in it. Loving my gayness and celebrating it made Satan flee. I had to thoroughly believe that my gayness was in Christ. I knew I must teach others that being gay makes them beautiful in Christ's eyes. These are the only eyes that matter. It does not matter what society thinks. Believing anything other than Christ's opinion of things is one of Satan's tricks. It's so important for gay people to realize that Christ loves them exactly as they are because he made them that way.

THE MAJESTY AND GOODNESS OF JESUS IN THE HEALING

•◦►◄◦•

It's almost impossible to put Jesus's goodness into words. The best way to describe it is radiant love. I would never have made it through this process had Jesus not revealed his love for me on several occasions. This occurred as I was battling Satan. Experiences kept me going. Being able to talk to Jesus on a daily basis kept me on the spiritual path. He was always there for me, even when my attitude slipped. The experience of God in the healing of my gayness has been the cornerstone of my experience. That he could bless a human being with the ability to talk to him directly is the daily miracle of my life.

Even when I was attacked by negative thoughts and feelings, Jesus was still there. He is always there if I just do my best. He is always there when I battle evil thoughts and feelings. I have to obey him constantly. I could tell my effectiveness by how I felt spiritually. Obedience would result in calmness, a sense of pleasure and joy, and a sense of satisfaction. This was the case even when doing difficult work. Jesus always made it possible to commit myself to doing good. It was not always easy to do good deeds, but it was always worth it. Words cannot fully express how childlike Jesus makes you feel when you obey him. This always requires work. The spiritual path is not a free ride.

There are no words to express the goodness of what Christ has done for me. I'm obligated to spend the rest of my life repaying him. He knew what was wrong with me when I didn't. This is the beauty of my experience. Jesus requires that I give up my self-will. I could never have guessed how repressed I was, or that my spirituality was so tied to my sexuality. When I feel attracted to another man, I feel closer to Christ. He is the source of my sexuality. He provides expanding experiences as long I'm willing to love myself. What he gives back is always more than what I put in. He is a generous God. Many times he has revealed the innocence of my sexuality. He reveals all the things that are beautiful about me that I could never have imagined.

Being taught gay love by Christ, and how to love in general, is more valuable than I could have ever imagined. I can't imagine anything better, outside of going to heaven. Gay people in Christ should be proud of the way they love. He wants me to enjoy sexual intimacy, but only in the context in which he created it—being in a loving, monogamous relationship. He showed me that all sexuality is to be enjoyed. Sexuality is supposed to foster a sense of connection, not a sense of selfishness. He is the director of all healthy sexual activity and love. Christ meant gay sex to be spiritual for both people, as he designed sex to be highly spiritual in nature.

For the longest time, I never saw sexuality as spiritual. I had gay sexuality associated with a sense of wrongness, but all that was being influenced by Satan. The cosigning of hatred of my real self was evil. It was my deepest sin. Given how strong my feelings are now, it must've taken colossal hatred to suppress them for twenty-three years. While Satan was the ultimate source of the hatred, I was responsible for cosigning that hatred by assuming it to be the truth. I thought I was inferior because I was gay. However, it was only after

I began to heal that I could experience the depth of my sin. This is how Satan deceived me. I never associated the repression with sin, which it clearly was. This is what happens when you're taught that love is a sin. I ended up with everything backward. This was exactly the way Satan wanted it.

In July 2012 I marched in a gay-pride parade and felt Jesus's love pour into me. The solution to a hate-centered consciousness is a love-centered consciousness. I'm developing that. It takes time to do the right thing. What I can do now is cosign the beautiful gay love that I am in Christ. It's hard to explain what it's like to not be attracted to men for twenty-three years and then be healed. I would call it a miracle. The question is: What was my role in this? It took embracing every single good gay feeling and then acting my way into my real self. This was the case even when Satan tried to suppress it. Love has to be sought despite resistance to it. The resistance to it in consciousness is always of Satan. I learned that I had to commit to love until I could actually feel it. The commitment proceeded being able to feel it. This is the truth of Christ, as with any work done before getting results. This is where perseverance is essential. This is where following conscience comes in. I knew I would not get results without doing work.

Hard work is a very holy thing, even though it doesn't always feel good. It's so good for the spirit. Satan will try to get one to avoid hard work, precisely because it is so spiritually healthy. Love is work and work is love. Serving Christ is working. Serving Christ is the reason we are alive. He is in charge of everything. When we work, he rewards us with fellowship. When we shirk work, we fall under Satan's influence.

DO IT WITH LOVE

Everything needs to be done with real love, which is reflected in actions and thoughts. Since Satan was always trying to prevent productivity, my solution was to perform tasks with love. This was the way to beat him. But in order for this to work, I had to dedicate myself to always doing the right thing no matter how I felt. Work was actually a pleasure once I submitted. Only resistance makes it feel like drudgery. Work is holy. Once submitted to it, it became a lot easier to do. Surrendered will is much more effective. Satan's goal is to try to get me to not surrender to the cross and to hold onto self-will in certain areas of my life. Actually, surrendering my self-will is an enjoyable experience. Christ makes it much easier to determine his will when I surrender myself. The question then becomes how to surrender oneself.

Read the gospels. Take up your cross against your self-will. Denial of the cross is denial of Christ. For example, let's consider when I know I should do something I feel resistance to. Happiness will come from taking that action. It is impossible to feel good after having done wrong. This is the case because our spirits are connected directly to God, who disciplines us in a loving way. My self-will got me nowhere. It was only when I surrendered myself to Christ's way that I began to experience happiness. I had to do what was right and not procrastinate. Doing the maximum amount of work gets maximum results. Each day Satan will try to prevent me from doing this, but I cannot give in to his selfish ways. My relationship with Jesus is determined by everything that I think, feel, and do.

Throughout this healing process, it is hard to express how blessed I have been spiritually. Jesus was with me through every aspect of getting through the false self. The ability to communicate with Jesus through his smiling is of value beyond words. I cannot express the amount of love I feel from this. I can't imagine having a greater blessing. Some of the things revealed to me are truly amazing. The time the Lord has put into my healing is beyond words. At times I felt his love all day long, helping me battle through the satanic hatred. It helps to remember that I am in a relationship with Jesus and that he cares about every thought and feeling I have. This truly changes the way I live. There is nothing outside of the realm of his beautiful awareness. Every thought, feeling, and action is subjected to it. There is nothing he doesn't deeply care about.

Given what I've experienced, I know Jesus can establish communication in a loving way with anyone who needs it. He will guide me directly if I want to do his will. The truth is I have to be willing to do his will despite my feelings. I can't act based on self all the time. I have to consider whether my actions are in line with the truth of the gospel. This is not easy.

The closer I get to Jesus, the more I can experience him. This especially has to do with my conscience. Jesus can guide me, and it's amazing what the conscience can tell a person. It's God's direct guidance. If something doesn't feel right, it probably isn't. I will sometimes have to do things against my self-will to follow my conscience. After all, I am a sinful human and don't always feel like doing what is right. If I'm not sure what the right action to take is, I pause for a minute and evaluate it from the standpoint of conscience. If the action just doesn't feel right, I don't do it. This takes practice and discipline. I have to remember that the spiritual stakes are very high. I have to remember what Jesus taught. Everything I think, feel, and do is being evaluated by God. I have to remember that I am God's servant. Servants are not lazy, which is what Satan tempts me to be. In terms of my conscience, God's guidance is very gentle yet constant. My conscience is my connection to God and his guidance.

One of Satan's tricks is to make me think there is neutral spiritual ground. He likes me to think I can make a choice and not have it affect me. In my experience there is no neutral spiritual ground. In my moment-by-moment decisions, I get closer to or further away from Christ. This relates to thoughts, words, and deeds. I am constantly shaping my eternity. I constantly choose which side to take. While this sounds like an easy decision, in action it is not always that easy. This is because I may have to go through some resistance. This often requires the use of thought reversal. If evil thoughts come into my consciousness, I need to immediately reverse them.

It takes constant effort to stay on Christ's path. It puts me in touch with my weaknesses. I believe every choice and thought is a battle. If this seems like too much work, get used to it because that is what it takes to battle Satan. This means doing things I don't feel like doing. The truth is that each thought and feeling affects my spiritual condition whether I realize it or not, and this is what determines my moods. It's not the initial thoughts and feelings that I have but how I choose to respond to them.

As I progress toward a more love-centered consciousness and spend more time thinking about Christ, I have to give up my self-centeredness. There will be resistance to this. Part of this process will seem uncomfortable. I have to suffer through this resistance to doing goodness. Once I'm doing the right thing Satan attacks me. Most people quit when they start to get attacked. It is important not to do this. I have to fight through resistance to doing good things. Sometimes doing good is very uncomfortable at first.

Jesus was willing to suffer, and he was God, so willingness to suffer for his sake is a holy thing. This provides me with more determination to do what is right. If the right thing always felt easy, then what reward would there be in that? Clearly suffering is part of this process. There is voluntary and involuntary suffering. Voluntary suffering is the suffering I go through when Satan tries to prevent me from doing goodness. At the end of this suffering, there is always joy. Then there is involuntary suffering, which is the suffering I encounter when I fail to carry my cross. The solution to this type of suffering is to take a positive action, to do something spiritually good.

WILLINGNESS TO SUFFER

As I progress more toward a love-centered consciousness and spend more time thinking about Christ, it begins to feel more and more like I am in a relationship with him. There is resistance to this. The key is recognizing evil resistance for what it is. Satan will make doing good things uncomfortable at first. This requires perseverance. This is part of the daily battle against evil. Nobody is free from this. Even Christ had to be tempted by Satan. Going through this type of resistance is part of the process. I have to get used to fighting through uncomfortable feelings to do right. Hard work will eventually pay off, but not always right away. If I do these things consistently I will be in a good mood. I have to accept that it is sin that detracts from how I feel. This is the reality of the spiritual life.

I will always have to persevere in life. I have to make myself do the right thing all the time. Jesus does not expect me to be perfect, but I do have to try.

THE FALSE HAPPINESS TRICK

In my opinion, Satan has the world fooled when it comes to the kind of "happiness" that it offers. This especially comes from the media. While capitalism is not evil in itself, the world idolizes material success and thinks it brings happiness. Jesus told the rich man in the Bible to give up his possessions and give to the poor. The man refused to do this and went away unhappy. In my experience, I had most of the things that the world thinks makes one happy, yet I was in the grips of a satanic possession. This shows you how far the world's advice goes. In my opinion, the only real source of happiness is living in an obedient relationship with Jesus. He is the source of all joy.

I have to defy Satan in order to do this, and this requires hard work. But hard work for Jesus produces intense joy. However, if the false happiness is all I know, then it makes it even harder to take this leap of faith and follow Jesus. This is especially the case when I'm asked to give up my self-will. I will have to go through the satanic resistance in order to get this joy, but it will be worth it in the end. Real joy comes from self-denial, taking up my cross, and doing good things. The emphasis here is on doing. I can think all day about doing the right thing, but it has no value until I do it. If my conscience tells me that I need to do something now, then I need to do it now. This is what I mean by doing the right thing. I learned that I could always read my conscience to determine what the right thing is. This is how God guides me. Oftentimes my conscience will tell me that I need to do what is more difficult in order to be happy, and I need to follow that. Obedience to God's will is most essential part of being happy and walking the spiritual path. There are times when I think I am on the right track, but my conscience tells me that I must do something different.

I have a choice to make. I must always choose what my conscience is telling me in these situations. I must try to sense the good in a situation and then do it. This is how I can make an assessment of what God's will is for me. It really is this simple. Most people tend to get confused when trying to determine God's will, but it really is a moment-by-moment thing. The key is realizing that my conscience is connected to God and that my conscience will guide me moment by moment. The key is being willing to act according to my conscience. But what my conscience tells me to do and what I feel like doing are often two different things, and here's where I must act according to my conscience. This is not easy. No one said the spiritual path was easy.

When I pay close attention to my feelings, I see that acting according to my conscience always makes me feel good, and this is God rewarding me. This is when I sense that there is something trying to distract me from doing the right thing. Why else would my feelings and my conscience be on different pages so often? Satan is clearly trying to get me to do evil. I learned that in my spiritual illness. Often I would wait until I felt like doing something in order to do it. This was Satan's way. I never checked in with my conscience. Thankfully Jesus has forgiven me for acting like that. I know it's hard to imagine going against your feelings most of the time, but that's what it takes early in the process.

Before I became more closely connected with love, I almost never felt like doing the right thing. In the beginning it took tremendous effort to start doing that. Thank God love is contagious. I had learned that sometimes my conscience would tell me to do something I didn't feel like doing, and I had to do it right away. This was Jesus guiding me. What convinced me of this is that the smile and my conscience were always "on the same page." When I act according to my conscience, I feel a warm glow in my soul.

Likewise I feel a dip in positive spirit when I don't do this. These reactions happen quickly. This is God disciplining me. He is constantly producing feelings and thoughts within every human being. I just had to learn to recognize them for what they were. It's when we don't think we are connected to him that we fail to recognize his awesome power. He can influence me moment by moment if I will just allow him. He rewards me when I do well and disciplines me when I don't. I used to think that my moods were just random. I don't believe that anymore. Moods are the movement of my spirit. Everything is spiritual. I cannot be a victim of my moods. I have to influence them with God through positive action. God will direct me in everything that I do. The closer I get to him and start doing things his way, the more he will bless me. I just have to accept that there is no free ride, and I am here to do his will.

PRETEND YOU ARE IN A
CONVERSATION WITH JESUS

I can begin to imagine is that I am in a conversation with Jesus all the time in everything that I think, feel, and do. One of the important things to remember is that there's nothing in the spiritual world outside of God's noticing. I have to have faith that God loves me this much and wants to have a living relationship with me moment by moment. This is a relationship I can feel. It is total miracle. He cares about me so much that I can constantly feel his presence in my soul. While all Satan wants to do is hide and trick a person, all God wants to do establish loving communication.

While I cannot be sure everyone will be blessed with a phenomenon like the smile, I can guarantee people will be able feel their spirit react in God to everything they think, feel, and do. This is the reality of living in Christ. All I have to do is believe Jesus has this type of power and I will be able to feel it. Jesus is truly Lord over all spirits. We are his flock. He loves us and wants to help us. I had to learn there was a practical way to feel his power.

The important thing to remember is that my spirit is not separate from Christ's. It is under his control and connected to him. He constantly lovingly disciplines me. This is an active, living relationship. He does truly care about everything that happens in my consciousness. This is something I acutely feel. It is possible to feel my spiritual condition shift over the course of thoughts, feelings, and actions. Strong positive or negative thoughts will cause more dramatic shifts in the spirit. Healthy thoughts and actions will be rewarded. Denial of self will be rewarded. Taking up my cross will be rewarded. Laziness will be punished. Selfishness will be punished. Negativity will be punished. By noticing these changes, one can truly feel their loving relationship with Jesus.

This is not an intellectual experience. It is a living relationship. That is what Jesus wants with all of us. This is when I truly realized I was a child of God. He cares about us so much that we are not separate from his spirit. I can feel in my spirit if I'm acting according to his desires. When I do this, I feel my spirit come alive with his love. This takes a daily death of self. One must pour out themselves in favor of service to Jesus because that is what he does for us. I must obey him at all times. It's through the movements of my spirit that I realize how intimate my relationship is with him. Once I truly connect to his spirit, I won't want to experience anything outside of his love. I have to deny myself on a daily basis and learn that it is not a free ride. I cannot sit on my laurels and experience the depth of his love that he wants me to experience. This is how one truly becomes a follower of Christ. It is easy to say I am a follower of Christ but much harder to follow my heart all day long. Yet in Christ all things are possible.

Once again I will have to go through resistance. There is nothing Satan wants more than to block my progress in getting closer to Christ. Yet if I am determined enough, he cannot stop me. This is especially the case when I'm trying to align my thinking and feeling to the virtues. I have to do this in order to build a relationship with Jesus. When I think and feel in accordance with the virtues, I can feel it in my spirit. I can live with a clean conscience. I may have to learn to fight Satan all day and night to get my thoughts and feelings back on track, but it will be worth it. It is not easy to change my thoughts from self-centered to virtuous. This is what Jesus bids for every person. Jesus said "take up your cross and follow me."

As I move forward in my relationship with Jesus through adjusting my thoughts, feelings, and actions, I see truths about myself I could never have imagined. I saw my entire consciousness was false. Satan is the king of self-deception, making me think I perceive myself accurately when I don't. He makes me think I'm something I'm not. A good way for me to test the reality of my consciousness is whether I truly feel in the depths of my heart to be a good person. My conscience will tell me the truth about this.

I may not always like what I see. I cannot begin to tell you how many times I've had to do the right thing while not wanting to do it. This is the true test of the spiritual life. It's all about actions. If I'm really going to be a disciple of Jesus, I have to do things that are good regardless of how I feel. I have to do this every time. The sounds difficult but is the only path to a solid spiritual life. I'm concerned that I was on the path to hell before Jesus saved me. I believed in God yet was totally disconnected from love. I did not act like a true follower of Jesus. I identified with my ego self all the time, which is not where I needed to be. I needed to be in my heart.

Then Jesus, in his radiant goodness, gave me another chance. For me the shock was seeing that I had murdered myself when I was twelve. Nobody had ever told me being gay was beautiful. Jesus has a way of revealing the truth. My real self was beautiful but was distorted by Satan. I believe everyone's real self is beautiful. Jesus will show me everything wretched that is covering up my real self. I have to accept that there will be tremendous amounts of work to experience my real self. I have to choose the virtues on a moment-by-moment basis. When I make the effort to do this, I will begin to unlock the beauty of Christ within myself. Christ truly wants to change me. I must be willing to do the right thing when the situation demands it, regardless of how I feel.

When I practice this, I feel something fighting against me, beaming negative energy into me. This is Satan. He constantly tries to bring negative energy into me to discourage me. I will be tempted to respond to this negative energy, but I must resist. When I resist it, I notice how persistent it is. My persistence in doing goodness must be greater than the evil. This is a constant battle and is not easy. Satan will try to get me to start by doing evil things, like being lazy. If there is anything I've learned, it's that I can't afford to take my foot off his throat at all, and that means doing as much good as I possibly can every single day. This is not easy. Welcome to the spiritual life. The rewards are greater than anything I could possibly imagine. It is often not easy to do good things. The easy solution doesn't work. What works is a determination to do good and to willingly go into the avalanche of hatred that is Satan. The unaided human will is not strong enough to do this. That is why a true living faith in Christ is essential. This is a moment-by-moment reality. I can do tremendous good if I'm just willing to do it with Christ providing the power.

A Gay Child of God

When I gave up my self-will and the false masculinity that went with it, a beautiful, gay child of God was revealed. This child was very innocent. I had to go into all the resistance and do all the hard work to get to this real self. That is the trick every time, to be willing to go into the discomfort of the satanic resistance. I can count on experiencing this every time I'm trying to become a better person. It is something that can be felt in my mind and body. It is Satan. What most people never realize is that Satan is this close in their own consciousness. He attacks me every time I try to do something good, with a feeling of not wanting to do it. He is selfish energy. This is where my conscience comes in again. If something is right, I must do it. God has blessed me with a conscience that will tell me the truth almost every time.

Jesus has a special plan for my life, and that is to do as much good as I possibly can. What I need to learn is that feeling this resistance is a sign that I'm doing things right. But before I do that, I have to realize I'm being attacked by something that wants to prevent me from doing good. This cannot deter me. This is where the attitude of being a servant comes in. If I take the attitude of being a servant, I will become much more willing to do good. After all, Jesus is God yet once took the form of a servant. This tells me a lot about God's character, and this I must try to imitate.

I must get in touch with how powerless I am to do good without Christ. The way I feel in the depths of my spirit is God speaking to me. When I string together positive actions with loving attitudes, I feel good. This is God rewarding me. My spiritual condition sags when I fail to do good. I must be willing to fight for it. I cannot adhere to my own selfish feelings. God calls all of us to be saints, and that means fighting against Satan. This is a daily moment-by-moment battle.

THE TRUTH ABOUT SELF WILL

The closer I paid attention to what produced the smile, the more I noticed something unusual, but something made sense in terms of the gospel. The more I broke away from my self-will and all the feelings it created, the happier I got. My self-will usually wanted to do the selfish thing in any situation, and this wasn't good. It wasn't in line with the gospel or the virtues. To be in line with the virtues was to do the right thing in any situation. I noticed that I very rarely wanted to do the right thing. I started to see something very evil about my self-will. It seemed to be always trying to block me from Christ. One important thing to consider is that society had always taught me that getting what I wanted made me happy. In my opinion we live in a very self-willed society.

I had never associated happiness with giving up my self-will. In my opinion this was one of the biggest areas in which Satan fools the general population. Everybody thinks getting what they want will make them happy. This is a lie. Being a kind person will make me happy. Doing good for others will make me happy. Doing Christ's work will make me happy. Most of the things society values, such as money, looks, and possessions, do not produce real happiness. The reason these things do not produce happiness is because they are not line with the gospel, which preaches self-denial and giving of oneself.

I had to see in myself that the selfish way was the way of Satan and that self-will was one of his tools of deception. All it took was paying attention to realize Satan was influencing my self-will. For a long time, I never wanted to do anything that was uncomfortable, and doing the right thing was very uncomfortable in the beginning. This is because Satan was constantly attacking me, trying put up resistance to doing what was right. This was a key in the process. My self-will was to be comfortable all the time. This led me into a firewall of evil, and in the end, it made me feel horrible. So I had to give up my will to be comfortable, and in doing so, I found that doing the activity that made me uncomfortable actually made me happy. All it took was giving up that initial surge of self-will and the desire to continue in my old lazy ways.

What is really important is that I take an honest look at myself and follow my conscience in situations in which my self-will arises. I have to remember that I have a tendency to not do the right thing, or a tendency to not want to do the right thing. It definitely seems easier to do the wrong thing sometimes, but it always leads to feeling worse in the long run. I can often feel it in my spirit when I make a bad choice. My conscience starts to eat at me, and I am overcome by bad feelings. While it is not easy to break the habits of self-will all the time, I feel better in the long run when I break from my habits of selfishness, laziness, and denial. I must deal with my sin. I have to be concerned deep down about doing what is right. Satan's favorite thing is to keep me in a self-willed life and then wonder why I don't feel good. It all starts with the premise that Christ is constantly disciplining my spirit. If I'm willing to give up my self-will in favor of doing what is right, then he will bless me with a better mood, more feelings of love, and more determination to do the right thing. I must pay attention to the movements of my spirit.

It was in this way that I was able to determine that self-willed living was serving Satan. I had to learn to break the habits of just doing what I felt like doing, without considering whether it was sinful. Granted, some things are clearly wrong and easy to avoid, but others are more subtle. This is where Satan can easily trick me. This is where my conscience will tell me the truth. As I go through the day and complete my daily activities, my conscience will tell me what is right. Once again the complication is that my feelings and my conscience may not necessarily line up all the time. Here I have to follow my conscience, knowing that eventually doing good will result in feeling good. I do not feel good by acting according to my self-will. When I start to make myself do things against my feelings, I feel better, closer to Christ, and much more effective. Each day in my healing I had to learn to push myself to do what was right in spite of my temptations. I cannot emphasize enough that this is a daily battle.

Each person's self-will will lead him or her to do different things, as everybody's sins are different. Each day I must battle to do the right things. This applies to thoughts as well as actions. If I do the right thing with the wrong attitude, it loses some of its value in Christ's eyes. I must battle to do the right thing with the right attitude. The bottom line is that I have to learn that self-will doesn't work. I know this is the case because that's the way I lived for a long time, not realizing it was evil. I must get out of bed every day with the idea that I must do maximum goodness in serving Christ. Anything less than this is displeasing to him. I cannot produce my own joy, and it must come naturally from Christ. This is how awesomely powerful God is, that he can lead me through my feelings. He will always reward me when I do the right thing. Acting according to self-will will get me misery.

This denial of self will not be comfortable at first. This is especially the case when I have been living in Satan's grasp for a long time. He does not like to let go of souls who are trying to turn to Christ. There will be major league resistance when I first start try to do what is going to reduce my sin. Again I cannot emphasize enough that this occurs moment by moment. I will see that my moods are not accidents, that they are dependent on me doing good. At first it may seem like I am constantly going against what I please. This will take some practice. I do not have to be perfect. Over time, following my conscience will make me feel good. I will see that the temptations to do wrong are hollow.

The wrong thing never brings happiness. Satan wants me to do the wrong thing so he can inflict more bad feelings. Christ wants me to do the right thing so he can bring me more joy. While it may seem backward that to deny myself would bring me joy, doing so will break some commonly held ideas. The first notion is that I will get what I want by doing what I please. The second is that denying myself will not bring me joy. This does not mean denying the good things in life. It means denying something that is not in line with the gospel or the virtues. It means going to the gym when I don't feel like it. It means not having that extra piece of chocolate cake. It means being patient when I feel like being impatient. Most importantly, it means loving when I don't feel like it. Each day Satan will try to trick me into indulging in sinfulness and drifting further from Christ. Each day I must resist the same temptations, as well as new ones. What I have to remember is that I am not giving up something that has any value. I gain everything as I deny myself more. I never have to deny myself love. But I must love myself in a healthy way. Denial of self is love.

I start feeling joy after denying myself. This gives me the sense that Satan is at the source of a lot of my self-will. I begin to see that every day, Satan is trying to trick me into doing what I please. Satan makes me think that doing things the easy way will bring me joy. He tries to make me think that doing easy things and searching for the quick fix is the way to go. This is where he deceives me.

In my experience, the right thing is usually the hard thing. It is not easy to be patient when I feel like being impatient, it is not easy to work out when I feel like being lazy, and it is not easy to love all the time. I have to exert some effort in doing the right thing on a daily basis. Jesus will never make this more than something I can handle. I have to get used to there being some effort involved. It is not easy to follow the gospel. It is tempting to think I can drift back into my habits of self-centeredness, selfishness, and laziness and still have access to joy. This is a lie. Each day I must continue my denial of self to retain joy. Jesus has designed it this way for the sake of my soul. That means each day I must be determined to take one hard action after the next when it involves living according to the virtues. The easy way just will not work. I know this because this is how I tried to live for thirty-five years. The hard way is the God-centered way. Jesus was God, and he did not have it easy in life, so why should I? When I start denying myself on a regular basis, my joy will increase, and then I will start to see that this is truly the way to live, not the self-centered way of society.

I learned that by giving up my self-will, I show Jesus I love him. My actions speak much louder than my words. I can tell Jesus I love him, or I can say I love him, but if my actions aren't there, then my talk is hollow and I will not reap the benefits. I can find a daily challenge in giving up my self-will. Surprisingly, it can actually become something I enjoy. This will truly open up the mysteries of Christ. As I let go of my self-centeredness in thought and action, I will feel better and better. Then it almost becomes a game.

How much of my self-centeredness and self-will can I give up on any given day? There is almost no end to this. Once I learn this makes me feel great and full of the spirit of Christ, I will want to do it more. Each day my temptation will be to do the opposite. Each day I will begin to see more and more that my self-will was satanically influenced. This can be applied to almost anything. If my sins are based more on inaction than action, I will have to focus on motivating myself to do things. If the opposite is the case, I must learn to resist actions. Either way, I get closer to Jesus every time I deny myself.

Do It with Love

In addition to denying myself, I must learn to do all my activities with love. This is not easy. As might be imagined, Satan knows nothing about love. Satan is essentially trying to project all his hatred upon everything else in the universe, and I am part of that. He wants to do this without ever being detected.

On the other hand, Jesus wants nothing more than to establish communication with me, and I just need to learn how to be receptive to it. Jesus did everything in his life with love, including dying for us. As I move from a consciousness of hatred to one of love, it becomes essential that I approach every one of my daily tasks with love. This is not easy. Nothing in this process is. It's more worth it than I can possibly imagine. The test becomes when I am faced with a task I don't want to do. I learned that if I really want to be happy, I have to start doing these with love. I can approach any task this way. Doing this turns tasks of drudgery into something I can even enjoy.

This is where the reality of taking up my cross takes shape. Granted, it is not a fair comparison to compare Jesus's death to a task I don't feel like doing, but I always have to remember Jesus's passion and death and how he willingly suffered for me. I have to remember when I don't want to do something throughout the course of my day that Jesus was willing to die on a cross for me. I know I'll feel better once I complete the task. My challenge becomes doing this task willingly and with love. This is where I have to do the action I don't want to do but with love, rather than shirking it. I will get nowhere by shirking work.

This is where conscience comes in again. If I remember that my conscience will tell me the right thing, what I need to do with love becomes obvious. I have to remember that it is Satan trying to keep me from doing the things I should be doing. That is the truth about my feelings of resistance to doing the right thing. Those feelings are Satan at work. Satan has the power to inject feelings directly into my consciousness when I'm trying to do a good thing. Sometimes these feelings will be quite strong. I have to persevere and do what is right to get my reward, which is the sense of feeling good about myself and the good feelings I'll have when it is done.

My mood will often shift when I know I've pleased God by following my conscience. I won't find joy and happiness any other way. I have to find it by doing with love those tasks I don't feel like doing.

It is critically important not to take on any task with an attitude of hatred. This is serving Satan. If I take on this energy while I am doing a task, it will be horrible. While this might be better than not doing the task at all, it is still not acceptable to Christ. What is better is if I try my best at doing the task with love. A loving attitude will make all the difference. When I do this, I see that my previous feelings and thoughts were from Satan, and I can do the task I never thought I could. Doing it with love makes all the difference. I have to work hard to maintain a loving attitude as I am doing the task, telling myself in my mind I'm doing something good, even if the task is not enjoyable. I'm always amazed at how my entire experience of the task shifts if I do this.

The other thing I need to remember is that love always takes work. It's truly amazing the way I can change my experience toward hard work if I try to love rather than resent it.

Hard work is always holy. It is one of the holiest things I can do. After all, I am here to serve. The attitude of a servant is absolutely necessary when doing hard work. This may not be something that comes naturally to me. The attitude of a servant is not easy. We live in a world that values being the boss. The only true boss is Christ, and my life's work is for him. I must resist everything in myself that goes against this kind of attitude. This takes hard work. I must learn to discipline myself to have this attitude on a daily basis.

This will bring me tremendous happiness. This is the natural reaction when I put myself in right relationship to the Lord. When I try to be the boss and control everything, I fall out of right relationship, and I bring suffering upon myself. It's really important to remember that this relationship can be quickly restored just by shifting my attitude. What I have to remember is that Satan is constantly trying to push me away from the attitude of a servant. This is happening on a thought-by-thought, moment-by-moment basis. Satan is always trying to push me away from Christ, and without Christ's help to be good, Satan has more power than I do. Maximum goodness equals maximum work and maximum love while doing it. While I'm doing positive work, Satan tries to push me away from it. This is in distracting, negative thoughts trying to try to stop me from the positive action I am currently taking. I have to learn to resist this with everything in me and focus all my love on the task I'm currently doing.

Satan will try to get me to think about when the task will be over, how much I don't like it, and how much I don't want to be doing it. This does not matter. What matters is that I do the task with love and think about how much I love doing it, even if it is a task I do not normally love.

For years I simply didn't realize my feelings of resistance to positive things were Satan's influence. I had to learn to go into the resistance and realize there was a power greater than me that would help me do whatever task was needed and do it with a positive attitude. Christ has the power to help me through whatever task it is that I'm trying to do. I feel myself become full of his spirit when I string together positive actions. My conscience will tell me whether I am doing an action with love. Love is not always fun while I'm doing it; many times it involves giving up what I feel like doing. This is the hardest part of the process. Satan does not want me to self-sacrifice for what is right. He does not like self-transcendence in my thoughts, feelings, and actions. What I have to learn is that self-transcendence will make me feel good, as does everything that brings me into closer relationship with Christ.

I have to get past the temptation to act on self-will. Love will win the battle if I follow my conscience. In fact, I feel Christ's spirit in me each time I take a right action with love. This is a feeling of comfort and love. But I have to take the right action and be productive in order to feel it. Each day Satan will tempt me to not do things with love, as he insanely hates love. But I am not a creature of hate. Love is my true nature, so I must take on love in each action. As I pursue the right actions with the right attitude, I will feel a feeling of love expand. I will realize that there is a system for feeling great, but that is not always easy. Being a good person and doing the right thing will make me feel wonderful. God has designed it this way.

Once I become accustomed to doing things with love, I will realize how much control I have over my attitude. I have to keep in mind that I will always pay the price spiritually when I shirk work. It is essential that I approach these tasks with love. If I don't do this, my joy will be greatly compromised. Attitude is truly everything. The more hard work I put into things, the better I will feel. The more activities I do with love, the better I will feel.

REAL HAPPINESS

In addition to doing more of my daily activities with love, I must overcome the illusion of false happiness. One of Satan's tricks is to make me think there is happiness in worldly things. He will try to make me believe there is no happiness in spiritual things, the virtues, and other things I haven't tried. He will try to make me think it's too much effort.

These are all lies. In my opinion, the world is highly taken in by Satan's ways in terms of the belief that money, power, and "getting what I want" will bring me happiness. This will only occur in the service of Jesus Christ with a pure heart. Satan will try to make me think the selfish and self-centered ways of life will work. This is a lie. Jesus holds my access to joy. Until I accept this, I will be stuck in a dead-end situation. Happiness is a byproduct of living a holy life.

The other thing to remember is that my ego identification may not even be my real self. This was certainly the case with me. It was this ego self that was so tied in to false happiness. For most of my life, I never thought being "radiantly gay" could make me happy. This was a lie. That is what false happiness creates—a false self who pursues things that are not important in the eyes of Jesus Christ. Serving God, helping others, and adhering to the truth of the gospel will make me happy. There are many things society promises will make me happy, and none of them work. If true happiness wasn't so elusive, then why is it advertised so much? In my opinion, the reason so many people pursue happiness in so many ways is because they are ultimately unhappy. The values of the mass population are shallow and do not bring happiness the way the Christ-centered way does.

I have to learn that I'm never going to be happy by putting on a false mask of society's values. Society taught me that being a radiant gay man wasn't the way to be happy. The truth is that it is the way God made me. By being true to this, I gain happiness. Often this is in the little things in life and by following my conscience. I must accept that I am dependent upon Christ in order to be happy. He is truly in control of my happiness as I can feel it. Society has no control over my happiness, only Christ does. The way I live my life is a barometer of my relationship with Christ, and the way I treat Christ will determine my level of happiness in this life and the next. If I try society's way of happiness, I will come up empty every time. I may achieve things I think will make me happy, but in the end I will feel no real happiness. This is not something I get with my ego self. Ego fulfillment does not bring happiness. In my opinion, nobody wants to hear that Jesus's way of self-renunciation and giving up self-will will make them happy. But this is truly the only way. With thoughts and false feelings, Satan will continue to try to trick me into thinking there is happiness outside of Christ. His goal is to keep me chasing false happiness as long as possible and convincing me I don't want to give up the things Christ is asking me to.

I'm being asked to give up the things that don't produce happiness anyway. I gain a better chance of eternal life and happiness in this life by taking up my cross. The problem is that Satan's ideas can get deeply embedded in my consciousness. Here is where the real work begins. I have to repeatedly practice the ways of the gospel and love every day. I have to work through the resistance. I need to go against what society has taught me. I will often feel Satan resisting me when I try to embrace ways of selflessness, caring, hard work, and self-discipline. I have to remember that it's hard to get to heaven and that the resistance I feel to changing my ways and trying new things is Satan trying to take me to hell.

If I pay really close attention to what produces resistance, I will see that transitioning from a selfish way of life to a selfless way of life will produce massive resistance. Satan's energy will attack me every time I try to do something that is unselfish and in line with the gospel. I must remember that this life is a training ground for my soul, and embracing the ways of Christ will truly bring me joy in this life and a better chance of eternal life. Doing the right thing is what matters, not self-satisfaction. I will realize when I start to become much happier with a selfless way of life that my selfish ways will never produce happiness. I will be able to feel Satan's resistance when I start acting according to the virtues. My self-will may try to block me from changing, but we've already talked about its dangers. To experience Jesus, I must do things his way. I have to act according to his teachings. This will produce real happiness. I will realize I have to start practicing this way of life every day. My spirit will truly come alive.

I will realize my happiness was in Jesus all along and that he was just waiting for me to start acting according to his ways to bless me with it. In summary, the way to overcome the illusory nature of false happiness and to stop pursuing things that make me miserable is to change the way I act on faith alone. While I will feel Satan resisting this change, going through the resistance will produce so much joy that I won't want to turn back. I must remember that Jesus is in control of my happiness. I was truly amazed to see the awesome power of God and how he produced happiness within me as soon as I did the right thing with discipline. I have to learn to act according to what really produces happiness, not what society has taught me. Society is full of lies. All real happiness comes from Jesus's will.

It's Hard to Get to Heaven

Given how hard Satan attacked me when I was trying to heal, I formed the belief that it's hard to get to heaven. If one takes a look at the Gospel alone, Jesus makes it clear that it's hard to get to heaven. In my experience Satan fights very hard to hold onto souls that he has ensnared. He wants to keep you miserable and sinful. He wants you to fall for his tricks every day. Most importantly, he doesn't want you to believe he exists. I had to be able to feel him attacking me around the clock to realize how hard he wanted to prevent me from getting into heaven. That is his agenda: to prevent me from entering heaven and to torture me for eternity. No agenda could be more evil.

If I want to get to heaven, it is essential I accept that the spiritual path is not easy. I must accept earning entrance into heaven through the way I live my life. This means doing all the things Jesus asks me to do. This means taking up my cross every single day. I feel it in my spirit when I don't. My conscience eats at me, and I don't feel close to Christ or have any joy. There are many times Satan has tried to attack me by making me want to take the easy way out. This meant being lazy and selfish, since these were my two greatest sin areas. For other people, his attack methods may be different. If I really pay close attention and put in the effort, the Lord reveals to me what my main areas of sin are.

These attacks are always in the form of feelings of wanting to continue in my sin. If I think I can continue to sin and go to heaven, I am lying to myself. I must be absolutely diligent to reduce sin in all areas of my life. This is not easy, but is the only path to the healing of my spirit. Christ loves me and wants to heal me. This takes a combination of motivation and restraint. I must act according to my conscience and accept that doing the right things will not be easy. I must accept that going to heaven means giving up my sin. This is not an easy thing to accept in practice. I cannot expect Jesus to forgive me if I will not put in the full effort necessary to eliminate sin from my life. There are no excuses to continue willfully in sin. The Lord hates sin. I am here to serve the Lord. That means every single day I must do the things that eliminate as much sin from my life as possible. I will be able to feel it in my spirit when I am doing right. I must accept that I will not be blessed with good moods and feelings unless I'm working hard to eliminate sin from my life.

This will often mean going against my will. It also means eliminating the actions that I should not take. It means doing this all day long so as to avoid sin. This is not easy in practice. It is not easy to get to heaven. The thing is that the Lord is forgiving when I make my best effort. When I'm making my best effort not to sin, he becomes incredibly forgiving. It does not mean that he hates the sin any less, but he does forgive me when I try. That does not mean I should shoot for anything short of the ideal. This is imitation of Christ. Imitation of Christ should be my ideal.

Society would like me to think I will get to heaven as long as I don't engage in mortal sin. Not making an effort to change my sinful ways when I know I am sinning falls into that category. My basic selfishness is enough to send me to hell without the grace of Christ in my life. Society wants me to think I can pursue worldly things and still go to heaven. Some people think it is enough just to believe in Jesus. Jesus was very clear that this was not enough. I have to live out my life according to the virtues and put Christ first in everything. This is not easy. It's not until I shift away from the cultural values and sinful ways that I will experience the true benefit of serving Christ and feel his presence in my spirit. I can expect Satan to fully attack me when I try to do this. This must not deter me. Practicing the virtues is not easy. I have to constantly motivate and deny myself at the same time. I have to motivate myself to do the right things when I don't feel like it and deny myself things I know are sinful. The truth is that God will guide me in my spirit every single time I have to make a choice like this if I just allow him to. He has this kind of awesome power.

I feel it in my spirit when I am on the right track. I feel love and peace. I feel joy. I sense his presence. The opposite goes for when I do not follow my conscience. That is why conscience is so important in this process. The biggest part about going to heaven is learning to follow my conscience. The temptation to take the path of least resistance will always be there. The temptation to do the right thing with a negative attitude will always be there. I must resist these temptations. There is no value and no joy in the wrong action or the wrong attitude. Joy will always follow when I take the right action with the right attitude. My peace and joy will fade if I take the wrong path. I can feel this acutely in my spirit. This is where I will truly learn that God is guiding me with his awesome power of love. He will not reward me for the wrong action or the wrong attitude. He will reward me for the right action with the right attitude. The catch is that the right action and the right attitude are usually difficult to do at first, especially when I have not practiced doing this. I must persevere in this phase if I want to go to heaven.

I can expect to be attacked by all kinds of feelings and thoughts to not practice the virtues, or to take the seemingly easier path. The truth is that if I pay really close attention to how I feel in my conscience, I will notice that I can always rely on it. God does not lie. My conscience is my connection to God. God's power is that awesome.

I must think holy thoughts. When I truly try to do this, I notice something evil trying to inject negative thoughts into my consciousness. This is when I truly see how evil Satan is and how much he wants to destroy me. I see I am dealing with a force more powerful than the unaided human will. I must remember that Christ is always helping me when I'm trying to do good things to get to heaven. It is not always easy. This is where I must reflect on the fact that Christ did not have it easy. Christ did a tremendous amount of hard work for holy purposes. He was tireless.

I have to be relentless in trying to do good things with a good attitude if I want to get to heaven. This is where I need to put things into perspective. Yes, it is difficult to practice the gospel. But I have to remember that the time I spend here on earth is nothing compared to eternity. I will spend eternity either in heaven or in hell depending on the choices I make while on earth. This is where doing the right thing with the right attitude becomes imperative.

If I take the attitude that this life is simply preparation for eternity, which is the truth, then it becomes much easier to battle Satan on a daily basis and do the right thing. This attitude will mean everything to me. It will serve as a daily motivator to follow the gospel and do all the difficult things that entails. I have to accept that it will be difficult to do this every single day, but this will prepare my soul for an eternity of joy. To a certain extent, this means selling out to doing what is difficult in any situation, as opposed to doing what is easy. Satan will always try to make me do what seems easier. It is imperative that I recognize this for what it is. It sounds easier to be self-centered, but it will just bring suffering, bad moods, and eventually an eternity in hell, which I clearly don't want. It is tempting to get frustrated with how difficult it is to maintain my spiritual condition. This is where I must accept that God did not design it to be easy to get to heaven. If it were, then our lives would have much less value. Everything would be much less beautiful. So I accept the way of the cross with grace and keep plugging away on my spiritual condition, which is dependent on my thoughts and actions. Satan will never stop trying to push me backward in making bad choices.

Now it's time to talk about deception. Satan never wants me to see through his deceptions. He wants me to live contrary to the gospel and go to hell. He wants me to be selfish. He wants me to hate other people. He wants me to suffer in this life and make it as hard as possible on me to do good things. He has no value for my soul. His agenda is evil beyond words. He wants me to buy into all the cultural values and ways of sinfulness. He wants me to see the evil in the world and be cynical. The truth is that I will only begin to sense and feel the goodness in creation once I break away from the deception of cultural values, worldly ideas, and anything contrary to the gospel. I must take the gospel literally. Once again, Jesus told the truth, designed everything with my salvation in mind, and then was willing to die for me. If worldly things really make everybody so happy, why is there so much suffering in the world? I have to really consider this and be honest with myself. Are the things the world fights for really worth fighting for? Do self-centeredness and greed really get me anywhere? I suggest the worldly values are the very source of suffering, as is anything contrary to the gospel.

Again, following the gospel is not easy. I must decide whether I want to follow the way of the gospel or the way of the world. This choice will determine my eternity. This choice becomes a lot easier once the deception of worldly values is removed for my life. For example, I valued heterosexuality more than homosexuality. I learned this from society. Once Christ showed me that I had to value myself exactly as he made me, which was beautifully homosexual, I began to experience much more joy in my life. This is where the deception was revealed. I can have these kinds of revelations in a multitude of ways, but I have to embrace the gospel's way of living first. If all I have ever tried is living according to the world—and of course this has not worked to produce happiness—then I will likely be cynical about a lot of things. This is exactly what Satan wants. I have to try to break free from sin and realize in the process that goodness of character and action is what will produce happiness. Society is tricked by Satan. Worldly ways will never produce happiness. Worldly success will not heal my soul or help me gain eternal life. I must break free. Satan will fight hard to hold on to my soul if he has me deeply ensnared in worldly ways of thinking and acting. This is where I must listen to the voice of God within me. This is where I must learn how to read my spirit. The question then becomes how to do that. Again, this has a lot to do with conscience. I must accept again that my conscience will tell me what to do, albeit very gently sometimes. My conscience is my connection to God. I have to listen to it. To break free, and to begin to act according to the gospel, I have to begin by constantly reading my conscience. Once I accept the God will guide me back to holiness in this way, I have to start acting according to what my conscience tells me. This applies to even the smallest things in life.

There is nothing that escapes God's attention and infinite love. I can feel this in my soul. This is where I also must accept that I am a spiritual being in a physical body. I must accept that God is influencing my spirit all the time. Sometimes his voice will be very gentle, but it is always there. I will face situations in which my conscience tells me to do something, and I must follow it. This is when I will sometimes notice that my feelings seem to go contrary to my conscience. This is the experience of Satan. He is the force within me that causes me to go contrary to my conscience. If I start to pay really close attention to the interaction of different feelings and thoughts, then I will notice this phenomenon occurring at all moments of the day. Sometimes it seems like clockwork, when my conscience tells me to do something and then Satan attacks me with a feeling of not wanting to do what my conscience demands. While Christ is ultimately the source of my consciousness, Satan is constantly trying to distort it. If I pay really close attention, I will feel two forces fighting. My conscience will tell me to do one thing and then there will be a feeling of not wanting to do it. Then I have a choice to make. When I follow my conscience, regardless of whether I want to or not, I will feel better.

The same goes for when I resist something negative. If I pay really close attention, I feel in my spirit the consequences of my previous action. This way I can begin to determine how to act.

While the right thing may not always be easy, I know my conscience is always trying to send me to a good place. With more positive actions, my conscience will get stronger. I must accept that every day I will not feel good until I take positive actions. There is no "something for nothing" in the spiritual world. I must discipline the part of me that wants something for nothing. This is especially true early on in healing. Satan will try to make me want something for nothing, or to feel good without exerting myself in any way whatsoever. This fosters an attitude of doing what I felt like doing all the time. A good friend of mine calls this "the dissipated life." I have to remember that I must take the attitude of a servant and do servant's work.

This is the daily challenge of living the Christian life. Yesterday's hard work will not benefit me as I try to die to self today. This means that I must give up my selfish motivations.I must do this every day. I must not get resentful about this. It is not easy. Love is not easy. Going to heaven is not easy. I must take on my daily tasks with a positive attitude and realize that I'm doing everything in service of Christ. Otherwise I fall into the hands of the evil one, and I will feel this in my spirit. What I have to remember is that I have a daily responsibility to live a Christian life. I have to remind myself the Christian living is about denial of self and taking up my cross. I must remember that Satan has nothing to offer.

He will constantly try to get me to choose the easy way. This means shirking work, or taking sinful actions. This applies to attitudes as well. I have to remember that I will always feel better when I resist sin. Fellowship with Jesus has to mean more to me than anything else, including my own self-will. I have to remember that there will always be a reward for taking the right action. I will feel the love in my heart when I do that. I will feel Christ's spirit descend upon me and make me feel better. My conscience will always lead me in the right direction. This may not always be in the action that I want to take it any given time, but in order to go to heaven I should better get used to following my conscience against my self-will. I have to remember how much Jesus loves me and that I am truly connected to him in spirit. When I don't feel well I have to look at where I may have sinned. I must accept that it is impossible to sin and feel good at the same time. Some sin may provide a temporary satisfaction. However, once I get used to the real joy that's in Christ, I will be able to easily recognize the sin cannot provide this.

Christ will never let me down. I feel a warm loving glow and a deep sense of satisfaction when I do the right thing. Conversely, I feel a deep sense of disappointment when I sin. Doing good feels good. Doing bad feels bad. The consequences for sinning are generally pretty immediate. I feel his spirit retreat when I choose a wrong action or wrong attitude. God does this out of love. He allows me to suffer when I choose sin. When I learn how to work for fellowship with the Lord and feel the joy associated with it, I don't want to separate from this. The difference between the spirit of Christ and the spirit of Satan within my body is unmistakable. Most people think these are just moods and fail to pay attention to the actions that may have led to them. I must pay very close attention to which attitudes and actions lead to certain moods. In my experience, these are not coincidences. To be in a good mood, I must do something good. It was not easy for me to remember this early in my healing process. While this is not always easy, it is the truth.

The trouble is that sometimes the right thing to do is the last thing I feel like doing. When a certain action or attitude brings the spirit of Christ upon me, Satan fights hard to get me to do the opposite. I will never forget when I learned that doing the right thing is sometimes the last thing I want to do. This puts me in a difficult predicament with a difficult choice to make. Welcome to the Christian life. However, the deep feelings that I have of not wanting to do something are often the clue that that's exactly what I should do in order to serve Christ. None of this is easy. This is where I must remember that God has every right to test me to see if I will do the right thing despite my feelings. Here is where I face my daily spiritual tests. Will I do the right thing? Will I do it with the right attitude? The thing is that it all comes down to following my conscience again. Doing the difficult thing will always have great value in God's eyes. Christ did one difficult thing after another in his life, and I must remember it is my job to imitate him to the best of my ability.

Here's where I really find out whether I am a real Christian. Why do the right thing that is difficult? How badly do I want to get to heaven? How badly do I want to maintain fellowship with Christ's spirit? What is my choice? How often do I truly feel like doing the right thing? How far do I need to push myself to do it? These are all questions I should be asking on a daily basis. The condition of my spirit will be proof of the kind of choices that I've made. Society does not teach things like this. It teaches me that getting everything I want will make me happy. This is not true. Making good spiritual decisions every day will make me happy. I will be able to feel it in my soul. My spiritual condition does not lie. Jesus is in control of that.

BEING HEALED THROUGH ACTIVELY LOVING CHRIST

One of the things I absolutely have to learn is that it is essential to love Christ actively all day long. He is my best friend. I have to believe he is always there with me in everything I do. It is essential that I not be mean to him by doing something wrong. It is essential that I remember that Satan will be constantly trying to destroy this relationship. Jesus is truly my friend. It really helped me to work on my consciousness by actively trying to love Jesus all day long. This takes a lot of effort. When considering there is nothing more that Satan wants to block in my consciousness than the love of Christ, I can be sure he will constantly fight me. This attempt to constantly love Christ will take a lot of work. When I make the effort, I feel something resisting me. This is Satan.

There will be times when I don't feel like trying to love. Again, I must follow my conscience and let it determine what I should do. What I found is that there is always room to love Christ more. He will always appreciate this. It is truly when I try to love that I will feel something fighting me back, trying to stop me. This is when I will begin to realize the extent of Satan's hatred for me and how he does not want me to experience love for Christ. I will realize the fight within my consciousness. I will really become aware of the truth of my consciousness. If I'm having a very difficult time trying to love Christ all day long, then I am probably still being influenced by Satan, and I need to fight harder. Love is also something that I build in my consciousness through my actions. This is where Satan will try to make me skeptical, or get me to take the easy route. There are no easy routes to loving. There are no easy routes to a love-centered consciousness. It is here that I have to resist the temptation of society to find a quick fix for everything. The only real fix for depression, anxiety, and all other seemingly mental ailments is to spiritually follow Christ. This means having to make a choice to try to love when it is difficult. Especially early on, Satan will try to push love out of my consciousness. The harder I try to love, the more I will be able to feel him pushing back at me. This is where the temptation will be to quit trying to love. This needs to be resisted. I have to fight for goodness. I cannot try to love only when I feel like it. My relationship with Jesus requires me to love when I don't feel like it. I cannot think of one situation in which Jesus would actually be opposed to loving. It is never sinful to love, provided the love is directed toward something wholesome.

This practice will be difficult at first. That is Satan trying to push love out of my consciousness. There is never a time when I will be most in touch with how much Satan hates me other than when I'm trying to expand love within my consciousness. He hates love. If I'm having trouble expanding love in my consciousness, then I must try harder. When I am close to a breakthrough of love, Satan will fight me. I will only fully experience this truth when I try to expand love as much as possible. There is never a time that Jesus doesn't want me to actively love him. The work is worth it, but it does take work. I cannot expect myself to just think about love and feel it automatically. My love for Christ will feel like a love for everything. Satan's attacks will feel like irrational desires to stop loving. I can also work hard to expand my love for other people in my consciousness. After all, it is Jesus's command to love my neighbor.

I must accept that serving Christ will require constant work to expand love. There will be times that Satan will attack me. I will desperately not want to do this. I must persevere and obey. Obedience is absolutely critical in the spiritual life. When my conscience tells me I must do something, it is essential that I do it immediately. Procrastination is of Satan. Hard work is of God. It is essential that I remember that I am a servant and that I take that type of attitude. Satan will do whatever he can to try to push love out of my consciousness. That means going into resistance and loving in situations when I would normally not feel love. It is in these situations that I truly take on Satan and his arsenal of hatred. Jesus will aid me if I work hard. I must remain humble and do things God's way. I will only experience joy when I am his servant.

Expansion of love in my consciousness is something that must be done moment by moment. It is essential that I work hard to expand love in my consciousness. Jesus will teach me how to love if I truly try. This means going against other feelings and turning them into love. This leaves very little room for negativity, complaining, cynicism, and everything else that is of Satan. I will truly feel his resistance when I start trying to love everything that I do. This is a daily challenge, because there are certain tasks that I may not have a natural tendency to love. In my case, I didn't have much of a tendency to love anything at all, but I was able to see that I needed to love more. In the beginning I could hardly even do that. Jesus revealed to me that there was a tremendous deficit in love from me. Initially trying to expand love in my consciousness was like hitting a brick wall. Satan does not like to let go of souls easily. It is essential that I remember that he wants to do anything possible to push love out of my consciousness. He is a pathological maniac that hates love. It's hard to understand, but it's the truth.

It's absolutely essential that I expand love in all the little things that I do. The other thing I have to remember is that love is not always a feeling. Love is often an action, and very frequently one that I may not initially feel like taking. I have to realize that is in doing the things that I don't want to do that I love. Love is obedience to the Lord. Love is hard work. Love is being kind when I don't feel like it. Love is having patience when I don't feel like it. Love does not quit when things get difficult. Love is living by the virtues. When I start living according to these truths I will feel Christ's presence in my spirit. When I feel lazy, I will feel love recede. There is nothing negative and ornery about love. There is no cynicism in love. Love does not involve me thinking of myself first. Love helps me remember that I am a servant.

This was the attitude Jesus took, and he made it clear that his role was a servant. This is the attitude I must take to join my spirit to his. It may not come naturally to take the attitude of a servant because we don't live in a society that worships it. Society values being the boss, having power, and being dominant. Such things quickly detract from my happiness. I truly feel the spirit of Christ when I take the attitude of a servant to the greatest degree possible. This feels like a warm glow that comes into my entire being. It brings me peace. Being connected with Christ is the ultimate joy and pleasure, and as long as I continue to live by the virtues and work hard, it does not fade. I must remember this is not a free ride. I have to keep doing good things and remain obedient in spirit in order to keep his presence.

Satan Masquerading as Self-Will

One thing that is really important to see as I get closer to Christ is how my own self-will can be deceptive. When my self-will is not representative of the virtues, I have to deny it in order to maintain my spiritual connection to Christ. In paying close attention to what produced the smile and my conscience, I started to see that my self-will was tied into Satan and his agenda. In my experience, Satan tried to bend my self-will often. This is a daily battle. I have to accept that Satan will try to influence self-will, and I have to fight him in order to do the right thing. Some days are more difficult than others.

So that begs the question: Is self-will evil? In my opinion it certainly can be when I act on it instead of following my conscience. It's when I bend my self-will to my conscience that I use it properly. My conscience will help me determine what the proper action is, and then I must alter my self-will to suit my conscience. Many people don't do this. In my life before Christ saved me, I used to just act on self-will all the time, doing whatever I pleased with very little respect to my conscience. This got me nothing but suffering and misery, falling into a deeper possession every time I acted on self-will. Again, it's important to stress that it will not always be easy to act according to conscience above self-will. Acting on self-will all the time is an undisciplined way of living. Jesus does not appreciate this. Sin is a constant temptation.

The problem is that we live in a culture that worships self-will, and it makes me think I will be happy getting what I want. I suggest I will be happy serving my conscience and doing what is right as opposed to getting what I think I want. I have to pay close attention to how I feel after acting on self-will. The movements of my spirit will not lie. Often I will feel empty after I act on self-will. This is not a mistake. God has not designed me to feel good after I act on self-will against my conscience. He has designed me to feel good when I act according to his will. I have to remember that my conscience is my direct connection to God. My self-will is often contrary to him. That is where I have to overcome the cultural obsession with getting what I want. The more I think that getting what I want all the time will make me happy, the more I fall into Satan's grasp and the more miserable I become.

Satan wants me to be as separated from God's will as possible, and embracing self-will all the time will get me there. In order to persevere I have to be very honest with myself, and I have to realize that I will go through major resistance to giving up self-will. The closer I pay attention to it, the more I will sense that that resistance to giving up my self-will is coming from Satan. It will sometimes feel very belligerent, which is his character. In the end I have to also continue to accept that he can and will inject thoughts and feelings into my consciousness. I have to accept that he will try to control me to the greatest degree possible by getting me to follow self-will all the time, doing what I please all the time. This is truly an evil way to live, and it will not feel good. This in my opinion is why society is not happy in general. Society preaches acting on self-will, not a seeking of God's will through the observance of conscience.

I can adhere to the cultural ideas about self-will, or I can find out the reality about self-will by paying attention to how I feel when I act on it. I have to keep asking myself the question as to whether I want a holy life or self-willed life. The problem occurs when I don't realize it's self-willed acting that's causing me to feel lousy or don't realize that Satan is so heavily influencing my self-will. This is Satan's best trick. He gets me to act on what I think is my own will while it is actually his. In terms of deception, it doesn't get much more evil than this. Satan's ultimate goal is to make his will and mine the same. That is why I feel so lousy when I act on self-will. How can I possibly feel good when I'm serving the spirit of Satan? In a fair universe, why should I feel good when I serve his spirit? This is where I have to get really honest with myself. While it may not seem to make sense that acting against my self-will will actually make me feel good, I have to consider that I am naturally sinful—or better yet, that Satan has been trying to distort my natural goodness for years. The proof is truly in how I feel though. The other thing I have to consider is that I cannot experience joy outside Christ's will. Satan does not want me to accept this. Satan wants me to think that I can keep forcing my self-will and be happy. This is a lie. There are many lies in Satan's domain. When I truly start to go against my self-will and act according to my conscience, I feel good. This is the spirit of Christ within me.

Christ wants me to feel good, but he wants this in accordance with his will. The more I practice this, the more I will see that my self-will was in fact the spirit of Satan. This is often a mind-blowing recognition. It was the case with me. Each day the temptation will be to resume my self-will, and each day I must give way to my conscience, which will tell me what is right. It's like a little game. However, the consequences determine where I will spend eternity.

Acting on self-will all my life will likely get me hell. This I clearly do not want. While I will never be perfect to giving up self-will, I must at least try to imitate Christ to the greatest degree possible. This is part of dying to self on a daily basis. I feel so good when I act according to the Holy Spirit that I will not want to go back to my self-willed ways. This is where Satan truly begins to lose footing in my life.

ARE YOU REALLY IN CHRIST?

Being in Christ is all about living a productive life that serves his will. It is essential that I live this out through actions, not words. It is really easy to say I love Christ, but my actions will truly determine that. Just saying I love Christ is not enough. I have to give something up, which is my self-willed life. The thing is that once I get past my sin enough to the point where I truly feel Christ's presence, I will not want to let it go. Every time I experience Christ's love, it so beautiful that it makes me cry. There's nothing that can express the beauty of God and the reality of being healed by him. Yes, Christ is still performing miracles all these years later. My life experience is a testimony to that.

I have to work with Christ though. It is essential that I realize I will endure attacks from Satan as I try to work on the path toward Christ. I have to ask myself the question constantly as to whether I'm really in Christ. The spiritual path is all about honesty. There are a lot of people who go to church every Sunday to feel that they are in Christ when they're not. Jesus looks to the heart and not to the exterior. As stated earlier, there is very little middle ground. I'm constantly either getting closer to Christ or closer to Satan. I must accept this for what it is. Based on my attitudes in my actions, I must always ask myself whether I'm getting closer to Christ are closer to Satan. When I act according to the virtues, I'm clearly getting closer to Christ. This is not easy. Nothing along this path is easy. One of things I have to be constantly aware of is the fact that Satan is a liar and will try to deceive me. He will try to make me think I'm closer to Christ than I really am. He will make me think in egotistical ways. He will create deceptions within my own consciousness. There is nothing he wants more than to push me away from Christ.

This is where conscience comes in again. I have to look at my spiritual condition constantly. If I'm being impatient, then I am not serving Christ. If I'm not loving, then I am not serving Christ. If I'm trying to do things the easy way I'm not serving Christ. I have to remember that Christ wants to constantly help me as I'm trying to move closer to him. There's nothing that he wants more than that. He is a lover of souls and a healer. He likes it when I take an honest look at myself.

I know from personal experience that the ego can be a total deception and that I must be very careful when having ego thoughts. My heart will tell me much more of the truth than my head. That is why I have to build a heart-based identity. I can say to myself that I'm in Christ, but unless I'm denying myself and taking up my cross, then I am not. Am I kind to people at every opportunity? Do I take the attitude of a servant? Am I receptive to God's guidance? Do I actively try to love God and feel it on a daily basis? These are the kind of questions that I need to ask myself to determine whether I'm really in Christ. Thinking that I am in Christ when I am not is the greatest spiritual danger there is.

If I feel resistance to asking these questions, that is probably Satan's influence. I cannot trust my own perceptions all the time. I had to learn this. The other thing Satan wants me to do is to never question whether I am in Christ. I must resist the temptation to think I'm going to get to heaven just because I'm not an ax murderer. This is total deception. I must take Jesus at his word and realize that the gate to heaven is narrow.

If the path I am on seems too easy and free of voluntary suffering, I am probably not on the Christ-centered path. This is how Satan fools me. I must remember that the path of least resistance never ends up in a good place spiritually. I have to be very careful when it seems like there is no resistance to what I'm trying to do. That generally means that I'm being tricked. I know this seems backward, but if I can't feel any evil resisting my progress the odds are that I'm not on the right track. The closer I get to love, the more Satan will fight me. What I have to remember, though, is that if I am fighting for love, I am on Christ's team, as Christ is love. I have to remember that the Christ-centered path is the way of the cross and that by exerting myself to try to do goodness, I get closer to Christ. This is hard work. While there may be times when I feel exceptionally close to Christ without having had to do a tremendous amount of work for it, I must remember that most of the time it will take hard work. Satan will try to resist me when I try to love. This is where I must maintain the attitude of being a warrior for Christ. I must be a warrior and a servant at the same time.

One of the techniques that worked well for me was trying to "find the cross." By this I mean trying to expand love in my consciousness until I feel resistance. Often I will not experience the full extent to which Satan is trying to crush my ability to love until I work very hard to expand that love. I can do this in all the small tasks that I do a daily basis. In fact, this is where I must show the most love, especially toward the little tasks.

When I try to expand love until I feel resistance and then go into the resistance, I am taking up the cross in the name of love. When I just try to feel love without trying to go into the resistance, it is not enough. I can also feel this resistance when I try to take a difficult action. When I do the right thing in a situation that is not easy, I am submitting to the cross. The cross is never easy to take up, but I know it will bring me closer to the spirit of Christ. That is why I must discipline myself to take it up every day. Taking the seemingly easier path in the spiritual process never seems to work, and I must resist this temptation. The easy path leads to suffering in hell in the long run. It does not bring me in touch with the spirit of love.

I really have to look honestly at how many times I'm tempted to do the easy thing instead of taking up my cross. This temptation comes in avoiding the tasks that I don't want to do, even when I know that they are right. While it may seem tempting to avoid the exertion of doing the right thing, even when it doesn't sound like fun, I must do it anyway. Then I will be able to feel it in my spirit that I have done the right thing. I may get attacked with thoughts and feelings of not wanting to do it, but I must persevere through these. Otherwise I'll bring more of the spirit of Satan upon myself, which I don't want. The spirit of Satan is negative, shifty, unharmonious, and full of discontent. If I really pay close attention to my thoughts and actions and the movements of my spirit, I will realize there are consequences to everything I think and do.

I am truly locked in a battle between good and evil. I have to constantly evaluate this. Then I have to act accordingly to maintain that I'm choosing goodness. I will not receive Christ's spirit until I have acted properly. In terms of spirituality, Christ has designed a completely fair universe. I must do good things order to feel good. There is no other way. I cannot force my way into feeling good, into being in union with Christ's spirit. It certainly is not always easy to take good actions every day with the right attitude. This is where I must evaluate whether I'm serving the spirit of Christ. I will be able to feel this in my soul, so the Lord will not make things too difficult on me. He is totally fair.

I must ask myself honestly in every moment whether I'm trying to get closer to him. I have to accept that in him all things are possible, and that I can get closer to him if I'm willing to work very hard at it. Some days may seem like a constant rejection of self-will in one thing after the next, and a vicious battle against Satan. I have to remember that I am constantly engaged in a battle of good versus evil. I have to remember that early in the healing process the pull of evil will be very strong. The way evil manifests itself in my consciousness will be different from everybody else. If I am honest with myself and follow my conscience, the evil within me will be revealed—or better yet, the way Satan tries to disrupt the good within me. The most beautiful thing is that I will be given the strength that I need to overcome the negative aspects of my self-will as long as I want to continue my growth in Christ. Many times the renunciation of my self-will will be in completing the little daily tasks that I have with love. The temptations will always be there to not have the right attitude when I'm doing the right thing. I could resent the work that I have to do, or be negative in some other way. I must resist this. I have to know that whether a person is in Christ or not is deeply dependent on how they handle the little things in everyday life. I have to do the little things with love.

THE FALSE SELF VERSUS THE REAL SELF

The deeper I go into my consciousness and start trying to practice the virtues, the more I connect with my real self in Christ. I have to get used to being a little uncomfortable doing the maximum amount of good that I can, and I have to learn to prefer doing good works to being lazy. I must learn to be a little bit uncomfortable as I progress toward my real self. When I try to change, Satan will attack me, so that I will return to my sinful ways. I have to always persevere in spite of this. Perseverance is the most important thing in the spiritual life outside of love, and it could be argued that perseverance is love. The false self is self-centered, and has a tendency to operate all day long based on what it feels like doing rather than what is right.

I feel this is unfortunately the way most people live in society—doing what they feel like doing most of the time without consulting their conscience. If I act and live this way, it is no surprise that happiness will be elusive. I must discipline myself to act according to the virtues if I want to truly realize my real self and real happiness

I must learn to develop a sixth sense about what Christ wants me to do in any situation, and act accordingly in order to please him. This helps me develop a new sense of what to do in any situation. It's called having a strong conscience. The more I develop this, the stronger I will build a connection to Jesus, which will produce true happiness. I will find that this true happiness can survive any bad situation I may find myself experiencing. I must not adhere to the characteristics of the false self. My false self was lazy, always seeking the path of least resistance in any situation. Real love does not seek the path of least resistance, but does what is right no matter what, no matter how difficult it is. The false self is ego-based and based on thoughts, not feelings. This was certainly the case with my false self, the one that tried to crush my beautiful radiant gay soul my entire life. The false self is always depressed because it is out of touch with the spirit of Christ.

The false self is selfish, always acting on what it feels like doing. In addition, the false self is unwilling to do the right thing in most situations. The false self must be slayed by the rejection of one selfish thought and feeling at a time. I must embrace the virtues as well, one thought at a time. It is also of essential importance that I do my best to try to control my thoughts. When I try to do this I will absolutely begin to notice the resistance and that I am often getting attacked by something outside of myself, trying to inject thoughts into my consciousness. I have to be willing to do the right thing no matter what any given situation. In the end the false self is misery. False self is what builds when I embrace society's values as opposed to Christ's.

Society values egotism and power, not humility and being a servant. However, it is essential to embrace being a servant and humility in order to be happy. I must try to do this on faith alone at first, because I will not see that in the world around me. I must act on faith alone at first.

TINY LITTLE SPIRITS

As I go through the spiritual process, I can sense being in a battle of spiritual forces that are greater than me. Without a connection to Jesus, whether I realize it or not, I don't have a chance. Satan's attempts to control my consciousness are done through my self-will, a false self, and thoughts and feelings that are not true. The key is learning to associate my self-will with the enemy when it is not aligned with the virtues. Satan is constantly trying to inject evil into my consciousness. It's not until I begin to fight these things that I realize I'm in a spiritual battle that requires constant hard work. When I go against certain things in my conscience, I sometimes acutely feel the evil energy. This is when I realize this energy can influence my consciousness but doesn't originate within me. I must not trust everything that's in my consciousness. I have to ask myself, was that Satan? If it is, I will sense his evil energy. I will sense that there was something evil attacking me. The same goes for when I experience Jesus's love. I will feel joy enter my consciousness when I have done the right thing. The hard work will always be prior to experiencing these wonderful feelings. Hard work is truly everything in the spiritual process.

No matter how hard I have worked, I will lose my connection to Christ if I don't continue my hard work on a daily basis. I will not lose it completely, but my mood will start to slide a bit. If I feel a bolt of negative energy when I question the source of a thought or feeling, I need to immediately reverse that thought or feeling. In learning to fight evil in my consciousness, I will be able to shift my consciousness to love-centeredness. I must believe Satan is the source of everything not virtuous in me. That is why I have to fight so hard to adhere to the gospel. I have to believe that Satan can masquerade as my own self. I've seen that this is the truth, but it is essential to see the truth of my own consciousness in order to fully accept that I am under the influence of these forces. Then it becomes an issue of choosing sides. However, it will take determined effort for me to practice the virtues in order to side with what is good. I have to try to align myself with God's will to the greatest degree possible.

The biggest thing that can teach me that my consciousness is not sovereign is an experience of Jesus's love. This is the most beautiful experience a person can have. In my opinion, one is more prone to having these experiences when he or she lets go of self-will. These experiences cannot be forced. I have to experience myself as a tiny little spirit in a battle of larger spiritual forces. This is the essence of what I am. I begin to experience the battle that's going on when I start paying attention to my feelings in the right way. Satan wants to control my thoughts and feelings without my realizing he's doing it. I will get in touch with this as I try to break my sinful habits. I will notice something in thought and feeling that is trying to get me to sin. Without Christ I cannot notice how much Satan tries to influence my thoughts and feelings. I will notice this the most in trying to do the right thing. It is when I try to take the right action that Satan attacks me the most. For me, this was always having feelings of not wanting to do something at the last minute. Sometimes when I take the right action, Satan will try to induce the wrong attitude. It is when I start to fight this negativity that I will notice that it is coming from something outside of me. Satan's biggest trick is making me think I'm not being attacked by him. That is how he fools me. I believe I am sovereign over my own thoughts and feelings when I am not.

I have to reduce sin in order to notice more and more the battle that is going on. When I am serving sin I tend to not notice that Satan is attacking me. It's when I try to break free from sin that I can feel the attacks. These attacks are in the form of thoughts and feelings designed to get me to continue in sin. This is where I need to adhere to my conscience the most. If I'm trying not to sin, I can trust my conscience. Then I can notice that I'm being attacked when I try to follow my conscience. Sometimes there is little very little delay in knowing in my conscience that I need to do something and having feelings of not wanting to do it. There is very little delay in this phenomenon. Additionally, I may also experience a pull of wanting to do something to that is against my conscience.

So this phenomenon works both ways. Either way I am in a battle of spiritual forces that are constantly trying to act on my own consciousness. I have to accept this I'm going to make spiritual progress. It's when I start thinking I have power that I fall into Satan's hands. He wants me to think I have power over my own consciousness outside of Christ's love.

HEALING IN CHRIST

I knew this would be the easiest yet most difficult chapter to write. I've been blessed with so many beautiful experiences of Jesus's love that it is beyond words. Jesus's love is amazing, tender, real, and produces a desire to imitate. Doing things with love is a good start, but I must approach everything in the spiritual life with love. I must approach the things in myself and others that I don't love, or think that I can't love, with the most love. Obedience is the key to everything. When I obey my deepest conscience, I heal the most. Everybody needs healing. Everybody needs to get motivated to serve Christ. If I'm experiencing something in my consciousness which is not reflective of the virtues, then chances are that it's probably not from Christ.

The problem I get into in my consciousness is when I think things are outside the spiritual realm. I cannot afford to do this. Life gets much better and more manageable when I realize it's all about Christ and not me, when I realize I am a servant and that I must maintain that attitude every day of my life. I must realize that I need to serve Christ in every thought I have, feeling I have, and deed that I do. It takes a great deal of time and effort to get there, but there's nothing more valuable than serving Christ. The deepest pleasure I feel is when I'm serving Christ. The question then becomes how to be an effective servant.

I must accept my battle with Satan and fight it daily. I must chase Satan out of my consciousness daily by trying my best to be a good person. I must know that I have Christ in all his almighty power on my side. I must know that Satan will flee from me if I do the work. To be an effective servant, I must stop living with a sense of myself running the show, because that is Satan's biggest trick. He makes me think that I have power when I don't. I will be able to feel Satan resisting me all the time, trying to keep me in my old habits of sin. He will try to get me to take the path of least resistance and not change. The path of least resistance is not the path to Christ, the path of maximum hard work is. Hard work is holy all the time because Christ put us here on Earth to do his work, not to be slothful. To be an effective servant, I must use the tools I've learned. These are using thought reversal, doing activities with love, being obedient and humble, and working hard to serve Christ. Above anything else, I must always maintain the attitude of a servant.

I will start to notice when I maintain the attitude of a servant that I will be able to feel the spirit of Christ within more strongly. There is clear evidence in the way that I feel. While being a servant may not seem totally natural to me, noticing how I feel when I take on the attitude of a servant will quickly translate into me wanting to serve more often. But I cannot realize the fruits of becoming a servant unless I try. This will not always be easy. Satan will always try to get me away from being humble, as it is a trick he uses with most of society.

BAD DAYS

Everyone will have times in which they fall short of serving Christ, and this has to do with disobedience and taking self-will back. It takes maximum work and maximum surrender to realize the spirit of Christ on a daily basis. This will be the case with many of the right actions that I need to take. I cannot afford to separate myself from God. I can always reconnect with the spirit of Jesus by doing some positive activity. On some days I will deliberately take on the activities that I didn't want to do in order to reconnect with the spirit of Christ. I must do this to the best of my ability. As long as I'm serving Christ to the best of my ability, I will feel good on any given day. I must let Christ determine what my best is however. I will not experience full joy unless I'm serving him to the best of my ability. The odds are if I don't feel his spirit within me that I am not serving him to the best of my ability, and I need to try harder.

Unless I wholeheartedly serve him, I can never expect to fully understand his mysteries. These are the most amazing things that I can experience. Letting go of my self-will feels very good in the end, and keeps me connected to Jesus. I must obey him in order to feel his spirit within me. Self-will will be a daily temptation, and I must never underestimate Satan's attempts to push me further away from Christ. Taking my self-will back is a manifestation of Satan in my consciousness. The more I'm willing to surrender to Christ, which involves doing the right thing to matter how I feel, the more I will experience his grace. It has to come at a price, which is the renunciation of my self-will.

The other thing is that my self-will is often not a representation of my true self in Christ. My real self in Christ wants to battle Satan and do good; it is my false self that is lazy and has a tendency to do the wrong thing. In any situation it is sometimes uncomfortable for me to give up my self-will, especially when it involves the breaking of deep-seated habits. When I break the habits of adhering to self-will all the time I will be uncomfortable at first. This discomfort is Satan attacking me. I have to accept this as fact. Once I have done the right thing I will experience Christ's spirit, but only after I have done the right thing. Often Satan will attack me as I am doing the right thing to try to get me to stop. I must resist this. Doing this on a daily basis is the path to joy.

There is simply no free ride in the spiritual world. I have to do Christ's work with a positive attitude. I have to accept that Satan will constantly attack me. Each person's habits of sin take different forms. If I am honest with myself my conscience will tell me whether I am doing the right thing or not, and what my habits of sin are. I must have determination on a daily basis. Sometimes I will have to give myself a pep talk to get myself to do the right thing. Doing the right thing works to improve my mood every single time. I must accept that I'm here to do God's work. I must accept that the tempter will always try to get me to do wrong. Being attacked by Satan is a sign that I'm trying to do the right thing, and I must accept the uncomfortable feelings that go along with these attacks. I must accept that the initial denial of self will can be uncomfortable, especially if I am in the habit of doing what I want all the time, which is sinful.

I must accept that this discomfort is only temporary and that my joy and sense of satisfaction in doing the right thing will far outweigh its difficulties. Initially doing the right thing may seem uncomfortable, and Satan will try to convince me that it is too difficult. I must resist these constant temptations to give up, and remember that Satan's agenda is to torture my soul for eternity in hell. If I learn to look at my temptations in this way, and realize that it will get more difficult to do the right thing the longer I put it off, then my motivation to do the right thing increases right now. I simply cannot act on my feelings all the time. I have to always consider what the right thing to do is before I act in any situation. If I do not do this there will be spiritual consequences. The denial of self actually starts to feel really good the more you practice it, because it brings positive spiritual change and fills me with Christ's spirit. It is only the initial decision to deny myself that is uncomfortable. Once I engage the right action I will feel it in my spirit that I have done the right thing. When I take the proper action in God's eyes I will feel his grace come over me. If I am used to sinning and am full of the spirit of Satan, this change will bring beautiful things for me. I must discipline myself to do the right thing. There are countless circumstances throughout the course of the day when I have a choice to sin or to resist it. With each right choice that I make, I build Christ's spirit within me.

I can feel this in my body, and it feels very good. It is the absolute truth that I will get a reward when I resist sin and a penalty when I don't. Self-will can be managed on a daily basis if I'm willing to give it up daily and not let it build up. Jesus is much better at running the show than I am.

Here is where conscience comes in again. I can start by judging what Jesus wants me to do when I pay really close attention to how

I feel when I think about doing it. If it is the right thing to do then my conscience will tell me that. This applies if I care about doing the right thing. If I don't, then I am already deeply ensnared by sin. So I have to first ask myself honestly whether I want to resist sin. If I do, then I can begin to trust my conscience more fully. I can test the validity of an action by consulting my conscience. If this is an action the Jesus wants me to take, then my conscience will tell me that. If the opposite is the case, then something will just not seem right. I must pay attention to these feelings. I must remember that God is directly influencing me through my conscience. I must remember that Satan will try to tempt me thought by thought, feeling by feeling, and action by action as I try to let go of my self-will and do the right thing.

The more I'm willing to experience the discomfort of doing things differently, the more joy in Christ I will receive. I have to surrender first and do the right things before I will receive Christ's spirit. I must remember that I am a servant. While the path of least resistance will feel tempting every day, I must remember that the difficult path is usually the right path in the spiritual life. I must constantly ask myself how badly I want to experience Christ and his love. I must be willing to go through some resistance as I give up my self-centered ways, knowing Jesus will show me the truth if I really want to see it. I must remember that the only thing that matters in this life is whether I get eternal life in the next. I must remember is not easy to serve Christ, but it is a lot easier than the consequences of sin.

I have to remember that Satan will try every single day to tempt me to return to my old ways, and each day I must defy him and turn to Christ. If this sounds like a difficult battle, that is the truth. However, the path of self-discipline and self-denial is much better than a life ensnared in sin. If I really care about my spiritual condition, I will be willing to do the right thing no matter what. There will always be a reward when I do the right thing. I will be able to feel it in my spirit. Then I will become more motivated to do the right thing and I will build proper habits of holy life.

When I'm willing to do things the hard way, things get easier. When I try to do things the easy way, which is usually the sinful way, it gets difficult and frustrating. I must believe that I can do all things through Christ, and then take an action that is in line with holy living. If I won't take an action, Christ can't bless me on any given day. I must remember to work hard at all times. Maintaining my spiritual condition is like maintaining my physical condition, it takes work. The problem is that most people don't realize that maintaining a spiritual condition is something that I have to do through holy living. I have to keep eternal life in mind all the time. I must accept that there is a price to be paid each day as I battle Satan. He will always try to push me back into my sin. It is not easy to resist sin every day, and there may be some days in which I will fall short in action and in attitude.

I must love God more than I love myself. This is what it will take to live according to the virtues. I must be willing to place the virtues ahead of my own feelings. I must accept that the spiritual process is not easy. If I want it to be different, then I'm not accepting God's path. If I think that I can take days off, then I am kidding myself. I must be willing to work on my spiritual condition every day by ways of living, working hard, and engaging in holy actions. I cannot want the spiritual life to be the easy way. It is almost always the difficult way to live according to the virtues.

One of the biggest tricks Satan tries is making me think I can get what I want from Jesus without living according to the virtues. I must embrace the cross as a way of life, embracing self-denial and hard work. I must sacrifice my self-will. I must change my selfish and self-centered ways in order to live in the spirit. I must embrace the way of self-discipline in thought, word, and deed. I must admit that I still struggle at times with sins. Even as I write this book, Satan tries to get me to avoid doing the work on it every day. Each day I have to resist the temptation to take it easy, and remember that doing good things will always make me feel better. If I choose to take it easy in doing Christ's work, then I will compromise my spiritual condition. This will bring suffering upon me. Satan does not like it when I exert myself to do the right thing. Each day he tries to make me lazy and skip my workout. Each day I have to resist this temptation. I must remember though when I sin that I jeopardize my relationship with Jesus. I must remember that I am constantly in a relationship with him. There will be days when I struggle to do the right thing, but I will be able to feel it in my spirit when I have done right and when I've done wrong. I must remember that I am not ultimately in control of my spiritual condition, aside from the choices that I make.

God lovingly disciplines my spirit, rewarding me when I avoid sin. Jesus will effectively give me the strength to do anything that I need to do, as long as I will put him above my own sinful feelings and thoughts, and let him dictate my actions. He cannot bless me if I will not do the right thing. He cannot bless me if I stay selfish and adhere to self-will. I have to realize that I cannot operate on my feelings of self-will and be happy at the same time, because God is in control and he wants me to operate according to his will, not my own. It is an evil trick of Satan for me to think that I can operate on self-will and be happy. I must resist all thoughts that make me want to maintain self-will. I must remember that ultimately my self-will will not get me what I want, which is eternal life with Christ. Only his will can do that.

THE BEAUTY OF FORGIVENESS

Forgiveness is one of the most important concepts in the spiritual life. I'd had a few days in which my willingness slipped, and I started to feel lazy about a lot of things. I became trapped in negativity and felt like everything was slipping away. I was not in touch with my real self. I started having trouble getting through my feelings of lazy self-will. I'd started taking the path of least resistance again. I felt like it was going to be really hard work to get back in spiritual shape. Once I became committed to doing things the hard way again, I felt Jesus forgive my sins and bring my spirit back to a better place. This was the most beautiful experience of the forgiveness of sin I ever had. Now the challenge is to sin no more, and to resist sin to the greatest extent possible. The constant challenge is to remind myself that the spiritual process is difficult and that the denial of self and taking up the spiritual cross will not be easy on a daily basis. When I want things to be easy I get in my own way. The easy path does not represent the cross of Christ.

Taking the easy path is the route of Satan. Taking up one's cross on a daily basis is the only thing that matters. I must trust that Jesus will reward me for carrying the cross, and I must know that I cannot balk at this. The thing is that when I'm willing to do the difficult work to heal, Jesus brings his spirit down upon me and makes things much easier, helping me to get through what I need to on a daily basis. Still, I need Jesus's forgiveness on a daily basis because I do not do things perfectly. The beauty of his forgiveness is beyond words.

Jesus's full forgiveness is dependent on me making my best effort. I cannot make a less than full effort and then just say to myself that he will forgive me. That is taking advantage of his love in an unkind way. I must consult my conscience in terms of knowing whether I'm making my best effort or not. When I make my best effort I can count on Jesus forgiving me for my sins. I have to be willing to fight Satan with as much of my effort as possible. This takes a daily commitment to resisting sin. I have the sense that Jesus will forgive me for so many things if I resist sin to the greatest degree possible. I have no excuses for not resisting sin to the best of my ability. I have to keep this in mind all the time. There are simply no excuses for sinning. Every time I sin I will pay the spiritual price for that. I will be able to feel it in my spirit. There are so many things that I think are physiological that are actually movements of spirit. I had to learn this about my moods. I also had to learn that I have to act my way into a good mood by taking good actions. There is no something for nothing in the spiritual realm. I must be willing to try to love around the clock and realize Satan will try to attack me when I do so. If I want to feel better, then I have to take a good action. Once the habit of changing my actions becomes ingrained, I will notice dips in my spirit and respond to them by taking positive actions.

A lot of times such an action will be something I don't initially feel like doing. I have to fight through these feelings and know that feeling better is on the other side of my positive action. Love takes many different forms, and one of these is hard work. There are many times that a better mood will be on the other side of the task which seems like hard work. Hard work is holy, and Jesus will ask me to work hard every single day to keep my spirit in shape. I must accept this hard work as part of bearing my cross on any given day.

FREEDOM FROM WANT

Once I start living a life of obedience to the cross, I will learn that Jesus can create a consciousness in which I want nothing but him. Jesus offers many mysteries and joys that the world cannot offer, and all I have to do to realize this to obey him with love. Feeling his beautiful spirit and his love will make me want nothing else. Nothing that the world can offer can compare to the direct experience of Christ's love. It takes work to develop a relationship before I have these experiences. I must place my relationship with Jesus above all of the things in my life in order to create the experience of fellowship with him. I must be willing to put down my self-will which doesn't work anyway. As was discussed earlier, the self-will can be Satan in disguise.

Once I develop a closer relationship to Christ and can feel his presence, I will want to keep doing the things that continue to bring me closer to him. Maintaining fellowship with Christ feels better than anything on the face of the earth. As I get closer to Christ, I want to pursue holiness more. There are so many beautiful mysteries in Christ.

Pursuing holiness takes a lot of work. It is also fun and enjoyable and life giving. I just have to discover that God is in control of all my feelings of joy, and I am dependent on him for it. My willingness to take the proper actions will also enable him to bless me more. I must remember that he wants to bless me and that he loves me. But I must also remember that I need to put him first in everything. Even hard work can be fun if I have a positive attitude about it, and believe that I can do anything in Christ. But I must accept the hard work. If I do it with love, that all the work that I do can be enjoyable, as each task I didn't like becomes an opportunity to love more. It's what I don't think I love that tests my willingness to expand my field of love. I will truly learn that I am on earth to imitate Christ. I do this by acting out of unselfishness, serving others, defeating Satan, and expanding love.

In order to change my habits, it requires that I enter a battle with Satan on a daily basis, and this means being willing to enter into some discomfort. Change is not easy, but is totally worth it. The pursuit of holiness in thought, word, and deed is hard. It is essential though that I not want it to be easy. The biggest key is learning to discern which habits are coming from Satan and which ones are coming from Christ. I must accept the Jesus will not be pleased until I'm pursuing holiness with everything that I have. I must also accept the Jesus will not be pleased unless all my habits reflect love. This is why I am alive, but I must fight for it. Jesus will not be pleased until all my habits are reflective of the virtues. This is why have to pursue holiness actively.

The problem is when I want grace without changing my habits. This is not a good desire to have. I must also learn to separate myself from parts of my personality that are not in Christ. I must separate myself from things that are not reflective of the virtues. This process requires a shift in consciousness in every way, and it requires effort in every way. There are some parts of my consciousness that are simply not real, and I must shift away from these. This requires hard work that I must overcome with love. I must accept that love is work and work is love. I have to be aware that Satan will try to reverse all the holy changes in habits that I try to employ, and will do this viciously and without mercy. After all, Satan is a pathological entity. He has no conscience. That is why I must show him no mercy when I'm forming new holy habits. It is critical to remember that I will not feel better until I change my habits to be more holy. Sin simply does not feel good, and it never will.

NAVIGATION OF THOUGHTS AND FEELINGS

I must learn to negotiate my thoughts and feelings as an interaction between Christ and Satan, and to see my entire consciousness is the interplay of these forces. One force that tries to influence my consciousness is loving while the other is cruel. I cannot identify with the evil and feel good. It just isn't possible. I must let go of this to the greatest degree I possibly can. My biggest problem is not letting go of the fact that these emotions and thoughts interplay these two forces. I try to align myself with a positive life-giving thoughts and feelings and defy everything else.

Fundamentally it takes giving up the notion that I have a sovereign consciousness. I do not have as much power over my consciousness as I think I do, unless I rely on Christ. The truth is that I am a beautiful creation, made in the image of God. However, there's an evil force that tries to derail my beautiful life and separate me from the virtues. The development of the virtues is the result of aligning with love and letting go of sinful thoughts, feelings, beliefs, and actions. To fully appreciate the battle that is going on within me, I have to be committed to serving Jesus in every way that I can. I must also believe that I am a tiny little human in a battle of bigger spiritual forces. If I pay close attention to my thoughts and feelings, I can feel this throughout the day. When I go along with all my thoughts and feelings on any given day, just acting as I please, I cannot feel the spiritual battle raging inside me.

It is when I start to not trust my thoughts and feelings that I realize Satan is trying to influence me. It is when I truly start to believe that my maladaptive thoughts and feelings are from him, and not representative of my truth in Christ, that I began to feel the truth about them. I must believe I have very little power.

I have to begin to believe that what appears to be my self is actually an interaction of spiritual forces. It is a battle in which I am an actual active participant, but I am not the ultimate power. Christ is the ultimate power. Nothing however will bring me closer to Christ than fully embracing my own role in the spiritual battle for my life. I must accept that there are two forces battling for my thoughts, feelings, and actions. I am not just walking around thinking my own thoughts and doing my own actions, but there is something influencing me as I do them. With every thought, feeling, and action that I take, I'm either serving Christ or Satan. This is why I must adhere to the goodness in my own consciousness. It is critical that I follow feelings that are reflective of the virtues. This will not be the easy path, like giving in to a negative feeling.

I have to fight that feeling and accept that this is part of my daily cross, that there is no avoiding it. There is no avoiding a battle with Satan in this life and that is why I am seeking a holy life. I must seek a life full of spiritual progress, because this is why I am alive. I must realize that I must work hard to deny myself and little things during the course of my day in order to live in God's plan for my salvation. I must accept that it will take a certain amount of effort to resist evil in any given day. This goes for resisting thoughts as well as actions. If I can learn to resist evil in my own consciousness in thought, word, and deed, then I will begin to realize that I'm in a battle for my soul.

It will be difficult to make progress, but I must know that I can do it in Christ.

In the battle to realize the beautiful truth about my gayness, I felt the attacks happen every time my feelings came into my consciousness. The vicious nature of these attacks made me realize my need for Christ was even more than I had realized. Satan is deceptive. Satan will try to get me to think that the feelings he is inducing are my own, and my fault. Deception is one of his biggest tools. I must not trust anything in my consciousness that does not seem to be coming from the spirit of love, as anything contrary to the spirit of love must be coming from Satan. My conscience will tell me the difference between the two spirits simply by the way they feel. Thoughts and feelings that come from Satan have an evil "feeling" about them, and he can inject thoughts and feelings directly into my consciousness. I must reject and defy these thoughts and feelings and the actions they suggest.

Seeing Satan's Futility in Myself

•◄o►•

If I pay close attention to how I relate to my defects of character, I will see some of Satan's futility in my own personality. Satan is always trying to project his evil on to me and everything else in the universe. He hates the beautiful soul that I really am. My futility was in thinking that I was straight for so many years. I believed so many of the lies and deceptions that Satan put into my consciousness regarding my sexuality. Because I was identified with the false self for so long, this shows how vulnerable I am to evil without Christ in my life. I am much more able to see Satan's futility when I follow Christ. This includes adherence to discipline, obedience, love, truth, and wisdom. Ultimately what has no truth has no power to do anything, and that's why the false self failed so often.

When I surrendered to Christ and accepted the path of discipline (which is beautiful), I started to see the futility of the deceptive path away from Christ. I saw how prone to stupid mistakes I was, including rejection of my sexuality and my real self. Drug use was also part of this. I had a tremendous lack of spiritual discipline, all the time acting as I felt like acting and doing what I felt like doing. I also lived a self-centered life, again acting on my thoughts and feelings without regard as to where they were coming from. I used to let Satan bully me constantly, without realizing what was really going on.

This, in my mind, is the biggest problem people encounter, which is not realizing Satan is attacking them. People do not understand the seriousness of sin. People do not realize that we must struggle against Satan, who is constantly trying to get us to sin, on a daily basis. Another thing with which I struggled was the lack of a sense of a relationship with God. I always believed in God but did not have a sense of his presence, thinking I was on my own.

In hindsight, I was being tortured by Satan, and he was the force that was creating this feeling of separation. The devil wants to keep me alone with all my thoughts and feelings, not sharing them with Christ or anybody else. This was a sinful way of living. If I'm not sharing my entire life with Christ, then I'm living in sin.

The other area of sin was belief in all the lies of my false consciousness, such as all the belief in shame and guilt about being gay. I will never forget realizing I was living in a stream of hatred and lies. When I start to feel bad, instead of taking positive action, Satan wants me to believe the negative feelings are the truth, when in fact all I am experiencing is a separation from Christ that I need to heal through positive action and thinking.

Another area in which I made stupid mistakes was in worship of my own feelings without judging whether they were reflective of the virtues or not. I simply followed my feelings and thoughts all day long without thinking about where they might be coming from, and I acted on most of them. This was a deeply sinful way to live, and I believe it was Satan's goal to have me never realize how sinful this was. You see, Satan's biggest goal is to make me not even realize he's there, thinking I am simply the source of all my own thoughts and feelings without any outside influence. The other area in which Satan had me fooled was in thinking about lots of things other than the service of Christ, which in the end is all that matters. Satan will try to get me to think about all kinds of worldly things and personal accomplishments without thinking about service of Christ, which is the only thing that will make me happy.

Another area in which Satan had me fooled was not realizing how deeply I needed to love Christ all the time. Satan will try to make me think that I can get by loving Christ just a little bit of the time and not in every daily activity that I do. Ultimately, I want everything I do to be an expression of my love for Christ. I must stay connected to this love in my consciousness all day long if I'm going to be happy and serve him effectively. Satan will constantly try to separate me from this love. Jesus's love for me is eternal, and he will not abandon me. I greatly increase my chances of feeling good spiritually when I try to love Jesus with my heart all day long. I must not underestimate how much Satan hates me.

The other area in which I sensed Satan's futility was not realizing how much Christ influences my thoughts and actions. When I try to have more power over my consciousness that I actually do, I am serving Satan. The other area in which I was fooled was lacking a God-centered purpose in my life. I must accept that Satan is constantly trying to pull me away from my God-centered purpose. Jesus will lead me with my heart in a gentle manner if I simply trust him and do his work.

Another way in which I was tricked by Satan was in thinking about myself all the time. These thoughts felt weak and powerless. Love is the only thing in the universe that has real power. I must accept this with all my heart.

ATTACKS FROM OUTSIDE MYSELF

It makes all the difference in the world when I can feel the attack energy coming from outside me, which means I'm not the source of all my thoughts and feelings. I must experience this truth in order to see that the energy producing my negative thoughts is coming from outside me. It is my relationship with Christ that protects me from these negative thoughts that distort my consciousness. That is what Satan is trying to do in my consciousness: distort it to the negative. I must constantly remember this and remember that this process takes hard work. When I get away from the process of hard work, I am in deep trouble.

I must take the attitude of a servant at all times, because it is the spirit of Christ that I want to connect with. My problem is when I think that Satan cannot influence me directly. My experience of thoughts and feelings has taught me that this is not the case. I am making a huge mistake when I think I am sovereign over my consciousness. This is how deceptive Satan is. It is when I think and feel that I'm the source of all my thoughts and feelings that I am in trouble. When I begin to relate to the truth, that I'm not the source of everything in my consciousness, I will begin to get attacked by Satan even more, except this time I will be able to see the truth. When I fight and transform my consciousness with Jesus's love and constant support, I see how I lived in a false consciousness, plagued by thoughts and feelings that were the result of attacks from Satan.

If I pay close attention to my consciousness, I am able to sense that things, both good and bad, are coming from outside me. Most people do not see their consciousness this way. I must remember that Christ talked about the narrow gate into heaven.

Jesus's Generosity
and Forgiveness

As I move through this process, I am constantly amazed by Jesus's incredible forgiveness and love, and his generosity in providing me with many experiences of his love. There will be times I will feel like I don't deserve the spiritual experience he blesses me with, but he is so kind that he will always give me a boost when I need it. For example, he has blessed me with several experiences of his love when I didn't feel like I was working hard enough, but he knew that I needed to experience this. The key is how I respond to his gifts. I can approach Jesus's forgiveness and joy of generosity with an attitude of laziness, or I can use this as a reason to work even harder to maintain my spiritual connection to him.

I must be rid of any sense of entitlement. I am entitled to nothing in the spiritual realm. While not all of Jesus's love can be earned, I must maintain the attitude of a servant in order to maintain my connection with it. I must respond to love with work and to work with love. The bottom line is this: I don't have to be perfect, but I do have to work hard and be grateful for everything that Christ gives me. The spiritual path with him is not a free ride, and I must not give in to the lie that I can get by with less than my best effort. I must remember that I must work hard on my spiritual condition at all times with good attitudes and actions. I must accept that the harder I work to be a good person, the more Christ will amaze me with his goodness in response to my efforts.

The key is my self-discipline. I must discipline myself to do good works, as my works are how I will be judged in eternity. I will not be judged on my intentions. I will be judged on what I do. I must accept that the path to self-discipline will not be easy, as very little along the spiritual path truly is easy. I must surrender to hard work. I must take the attitude of a servant and do servants' work. I must accept that the self-centered path will not work for me and will not keep me in touch with the Holy Spirit.

MISTAKES

The other thing I must deal with is when my work ethic slides a bit. This will lead to a loss of joy in my life. You see, working for Christ is my only source of joy. It is the only way I will receive joy in my life. Satan will constantly try to trick me into thinking that working for Christ a burden and that I should be sinful and lazy or have a poor attitude about the work that Jesus has put in front of me on any given day. Like everything else that Satan tries to do, this is a massive lie. The truth is that there is massive joy in doing work for Christ. I have to remember that is an honor and a privilege to do Christ's work every day, even if it isn't easy.

I have to remember that Satan will attack me as I try to do the work, trying to make me think it is too much of a burden to do. I must resist sin to the greatest degree I possibly can. My sin is often the attitude of shirking work. Sometimes when I make myself do the work, my attitude is still not where it needs to be. I must accept that Satan will always try to pull me back into sin. He will try to make me resent the work that I have to do for Christ. This will be a daily battle. I must choose Christ over my self-will to be lazy. When I serve myself I am serving Satan. Misery consists in choosing self over Christ, and joy consists of choosing Christ over self. This is the case because I don't produce my own joy. Christ produces it when I do his will.

Christ will provide my joy when I do his work. When I don't do his work, I lose my joy. When I take up my cross again, my joy returns. Taking up my cross means doing the things that I need to do and fighting through the attacks to not do them. I must remember that doing what I don't feel like doing will always make me feel good because it requires self-discipline.

I must also accept that Satan will always try to derail me when I get on the path of self-discipline. Satan will always try to stop me from doing good works, and try to make me return to my undisciplined path of self-will. It is essential that I take the attitude of a servant in every situation, because if I don't, then I will cut myself off from Christ's spirit. I must obey Christ. I will feel his spirit every time I deny myself. In the end I will see that I don't want my self-will. It will come to a point where I actually feel like doing the things I usually don't want to do, because this will help me pull closer to Christ. I will realize that I need to sell out to Jesus at every chance that I get. I will see that this is the only way to live. Everything will come together if I take the attitude of a cheerful servant. It doesn't matter what a single human being thinks about me, but what matters is how I appear in Christ's eyes. This means that I have to do his work in order to connect to Christ in the spirit.

I must also understand that Jesus will always provide actions that lead to my real self. If I do live on good faith, I will take on my real self. I must pray and pay close attention to Satan's attacks. Then I must do exactly what he doesn't want me to do. This is how I build self-discipline. Remembering that God's will is the only way I can truly experience my real self is critical, because otherwise I will identify with the things that do not bring me into accord with it. Sometimes my biggest sin is avoiding the resistance that I have to go through as

I do work. But I must surrender myself to the process and keep my feet moving even when I don't want to.

Hard work will always pay off. Self-denial will always pay off. One of the biggest struggles is selling out as much as possible for Christ every day. If I'm feeling less connected to my real self, I have gone backward, and if I'm having fewer experiences of Christ's love, I have let him down. I must run this race now by dying to self every day, and separating from the feelings that are not representative of my true self in Christ.

The first thing I must adhere to is unselfishness. I must remember all the time Christ lived a perfectly unselfish life, dying on the cross to redeem humanity. The other thing I must adhere to is hard work for others. My original sin makes me selfish and sometimes not want to work hard for others, but I must resist this. I must never forget the supreme value of what Christ has done for me, and what my life in him represents. If I'm willing to sacrifice for him every day and to die to self, then this means removing myself from everything not of the virtues. I cannot connect with Christ in the spirit while shirking work. I must practice self-discipline. Then I must practice humility. Then I must humbly rely on Christ. I must be willing to suffer through Satan's attacks to do Christ's work. This often means doing things that may seem a little distasteful to me.

ACTIONS TURNING TO MOODS

It is important that I allow Jesus to control my moods when I serve him with the right actions. Many people rely on their moods to determine their actions. This will result in my doing what I feel like doing, and not doing what I don't feel like doing. This is sinful, and I lived this way for thirty-five years. If I commit to being in charge of my actions and my attitude about those actions, then I can start avoiding sinfulness more. This will often require doing the opposite of what I feel like doing. This will be very uncomfortable at first, and self-discipline is the key. Once I take a right action with a positive attitude, I feel Jesus bring me to a better mood. This is how moods work. Moods come from Jesus when he sees fit, but I will be amazed at how often he will bring a good mood upon me when I start serving properly and with diligence.

I must accept that my actions will determine my moods, not vice versa. This is a hard adjustment at first, because the habit of letting my moods determine my actions is a tough one to break. I must accept that this is possible. This is where obedience to Christ comes into play, as he is the only source of sustained joy in the universe. I must not try to do things my way. I must accept that I can act my way into a good mood and that good moods are dependent upon good actions. In this way God is totally fair, but I must accept that there will be some work required. If I really think about it, living in a fair universe, spiritually speaking, would be dependent on my doing something good in order to feel good. The people who do the most good should feel the best. This is the truth in regard to my spiritual condition. Nothing escapes God's noticing, and my thoughts and actions fall under that category.

WORK IS LOVE

It is essential that I accept that love is work in my life. There is nothing more critical to love than working on it. It takes exertion to love. The last thing Satan wants me to do his work hard on love. He wants to keep me lazy and cynical. I must also accept that my love is going to be judged by my actions, not by what I say I'm going to do, or not when I think about doing. Love is not always a feeling, and the hard work side of love is not always pleasant. Oftentimes it takes a great deal of exertion that I may not necessarily feel like doing, but I always will feel better on the other side of that exertion. What Satan wants is for me to never try to love, or to engage in self-sacrifice in any way. When I am going through my day, I have to take an honest look at myself and see whether a thought or feeling is representative of the virtues or not. If it isn't, that is from Satan and needs to be rejected. This will take a great deal of effort sometimes, but I must remember that when I don't feel like doing something that's an indication I need to do it the most.

Satan will often try to get me to avoid work and be lazy. In my opinion, laziness is one of the most subtle of sins. I must not forget that Christ will help me as I'm trying to get the work done that I need to do, and he will fill me with his spirit as I'm doing it. Satan will try to make me shifty, confused, and unwilling to do the work I need to do. What I have to do is recognize the satanic energy for

132

what it is and persevere through it. Perseverance is the definite key when doing work. I cannot live a Christian life without a deep level of perseverance. Satan will always try to get me to stop doing what I need to do, but I need to persevere anyway. While Satan is stronger than the unaided human will, Christ's power is available when I choose to fight Satan.

The key to doing work and to loving is realizing that it's Christ's power that is enabling me to do it. When I choose to block a negative thought or feeling or choose to produce a positive thought or feeling, it is Christ's power that enables me to get the job done. My self-will takes the choice to go in either direction, but it is Christ's power that produces the result. He is the source of all power. I must accept that all power in my consciousness comes from Christ and that he gives me the power to get work done. If I take the attitude of submission to his power while I am doing work, then I can do it with love effectively. I must also accept that Satan will be constantly trying to undermine the good works that I do by making me not feel like doing them. He will use extreme trickery and malice in this way. I must pay attention to how I feel though when I complete my work. I must also pay attention to how I feel as I'm doing it, and how close I feel to the Lord. He wants me to live a holy life, and I must approach work as something holy.

QUESTIONS ABOUT CONSCIOUSNESS

Now that we have talked about some of the problems in consciousness in terms of Satan, it is essential to move forward into asking questions about a Christ-centered consciousness. All of us struggle with problems in our consciousness, such as depression, anxiety, anger, and other things that are not reflective of the virtues. These problems exist because Satan exists. The truth is that Satan is the source of all problems in my consciousness, but he fools me into believing that my consciousness is sovereign. I experienced these problems in my consciousness and did not realize for many years that the solution was a relationship with Christ and that outside of Christ I can have no joy.

Many people have learned the wrong habits of thinking and consciousness; following the teachings of Christ is the only way to a better consciousness. What Christ requires seems unusual from a selfish perspective, but it makes total sense in his eyes. The truth of human consciousness is that Christ is protecting us against Satan all the time. I cannot heal the false with the false, so I must get deeper into the depths of my soul to begin to disassociate from whatever Satan has distorted. What I experience as a normal consciousness includes a satanic distortion that is pure evil, and I must realize that my soul is much more beautiful than I could've ever realized. That is the truth of my consciousness.

When I have gotten closest to my deepest level of soul, I find splendor. This is one of the most amazing feelings there is. This is where I will find Christ. I have to get through all the satanic hatred to get to that level of my soul first. Satan does not want me to do the work to get to that point. He does not want me to give up my self-will over and over again in order to follow the will of God. He does not want me to realize the will of God is the only thing that matters in my life. He does not want me to see the beauty of truth, or realize other people have beautiful souls as well. It's hard to describe the beauty of my soul when I experience it at a deep level. It's hard to explain many of the things that are so beautiful in Christ. What I experience about myself is a deep level of innocence. That is why Satan hates my soul so much, because it is so beautiful to its core. I have to resist sin to get to this core. St. Teresa of Avila talks a lot about this in her book *The Interior Castle*. The closer I get to the truth of my soul, the more Satan will fight me. He hates my soul in all its beauty, but I have to resist sin in order to see the full beauty of myself.

For most of my life, I was not able to experience the truth and beauty of my soul, because Satan repressed it. I think in my heart Satan was scared of my real self, because it is in Christ. There is a creativity and diversity to my soul, and deep love that cannot be expressed in words. That is why I am so beautiful at my core. I mean this in a nonegotistical kind of way. As soon as ego enters the picture we have again entered the world of Satan. I'm talking about my soul at its deepest core, my indwelling Christ. I am a very gentle boy at heart, and very innocent. My spiritual experiences have showed me that I'm not necessarily even my thoughts and my feelings, but the Christ-centered soul underneath that Satan could never fully kill. Is truly amazing to experience things in this way, and I am convinced that I am extraordinarily blessed to have seen it. I know that when other people see their own souls in this way they will never be the same. The key to all this is putting Christ at the center of your life. When I serve Christ first, I get more in touch with my indwelling Christ.

I fought Christ most of my life by not accepting the beauty of my gayness. I love the energy that I am, which is extraordinarily beautiful, but not in an "ego sense." There is very little room for ego in a true relationship with Christ. As was the case with me, I had to see that my ego was false. My true self is beautiful beyond words because it is so closely tied to Christ. I get a deep sense from paying close attention to my soul that normal consciousness is not necessarily what I am, but the truth is my soul is my consciousness. I cannot get close to my real consciousness unless I'm in touch with my heart and with love. The bottom line is that I have to accept that my soul, and not my day-to-day thinking, is the truth about myself. However, my day-to-day thinking and feeling is where I negotiate the battle with Satan and get closer to Christ's truth. I also need to ask myself some questions about my own consciousness in order to get more centered in the truth.

The first question I need to ask myself is whether I am the source of my own consciousness. If I was, then would I be able to control my feelings? If I really am the source of my own consciousness, why don't I have the power to feel the way I want to all the time? Clearly I am not the source of my own consciousness, but Christ is. The closer I get to God in my own consciousness, the more I will see that my ego self does not exist in the way I think it does. Satan likes to use it against me to make me think I am sovereign over my own consciousness. If this were truly the case, however, why would depression and anxiety exist? I must question how something like this relates to my spiritual condition. Clearly there are problems, and thinking I have power over my own consciousness is part of that problem.

Another thing that I must accept is the problem of associating with my own mind all the time. This is especially the case since Satan can masquerade so easily as the ego self. I must realize I cannot trust my mind most of the time when I'm thinking in terms of ego. I must realize I can trust my heart much more than my mind, and my heart is more closely connected to Christ. I must realize that my mind can certainly be a trap at times. My heart is much more humble than my mind, and that is why I can rely on it much more. Society does not want to accept that the ego self is the enemy, a fictional creation of Satan, and tied into his ways. Unfortunately, society lives off ego. Ego is the enemy, not something to serve. I am a servant. This takes a great deal of self-discipline. Satan will come after me twice as hard when I try to take on the attitude of a servant, trying to push me back into an ego state. Ego is the devil's world. This is where the denial of self comes in, which is one of the main things Jesus preached. I must accept that I must deny myself on a daily basis. More importantly, I must deny my ego what it craves, knowing that this is probably out of line with my real self, which craves humble love.

I must accept that it will not be easy to deny my ego at first, to stay out of my head. Satan devours a head-centered consciousness. My heart is much more stable than my head, but I must learn to rely on this in order to figure that out. I must learn that I can actually think with my heart, that this is entirely possible. This is where all the power is. My head has little power to exert its will over anything,. It is important that I pay close attention to my spirit when consulting my heart on anything. My heart is also my safe place to run from attacks. If I pay close attention to the consciousness in my heart, I will feel radiant love directing me at all times. One of the biggest reasons I used drugs for so many years was that I was running away from the chaos of thought. Once I realized that I could rely on my heart, I knew everything was going to be okay.

Another thing I must pay close attention to and ask myself questions about is how my spirit reacts to the different thoughts and feelings that I have. If I pay close attention to my spirit, I can feel its reaction to different thoughts and feelings. Gentle loving thoughts bring a warm glow. Evil thoughts bring shiftiness. If I pay really close attention, I realize there are consequences to my thoughts, feelings, and actions. I can feel these consequences in my spirit, in my entire body. God is truly in control of everything. He can truly influence everything that I do at all times. He can guide me out of love in all ways. He can bring thoughts and feelings into my consciousness that lead me in the direction of his will.

Another thing I must consider is whether God values things in consciousness that man does not value. The truth is that God values a lot of things man doesn't, like being a servant. God is all powerful, and I have to meet his conditions in order to feel well on any given day and be effective. But what am I trying to be effective for? I must accept that I have to meet God's conditions, with the attitude that he wants me to have.

Another thing I need to think about and ask myself questions about is whether I have been trained by society to think in a way that contradicts God's values. For example, it values many things associated with the serving of self. In many ways, society values getting what I want and having everything my way. This is not in line with the gospel. Selfishness is the way of Satan. I must accept that I will learn misery from society, not joy. True joy is in serving Christ, not in getting everything that I want out of life and the world. I must learn that my only real joy is in living out the gospel, and living in ways in which I deny myself rather than seek to please myself all the time. Self-denial is my joy. I will gain massive joy by doing the things that I don't feel like doing in service of Christ. I must be diligent at all times in my work. I must reject the cultural worldly values, and realize that Christ will show me everything I need to know about how to live.

All these questions are legitimate about human consciousness. What if there was something that could give me the keys to happiness? I must understand I will not find happiness in the ways of the world. But where will I find happiness? The answer is centering my consciousness in Jesus Christ. This means moving away from Satan and his influence. This takes time and effort, denial of selfish ways, and paying close attention to my thoughts and feelings for deception. Christ is the only way to happiness. Living and acting according to the gospel is the only way to happiness.

The question I must ask myself is whether the world's teachings on how to attain happiness are wrong. The world tells me that getting everything I want will make me happy. The world tells me that happiness is in money, possessions, and similar things. This is a lie. True happiness comes in taking up my cross for Christ. True happiness comes in denial of self. True happiness comes in self-discipline. True happiness comes in humility. By embracing these virtues, I will keep myself in touch with Christ's spirit. The truth is that anyone can find happiness in Jesus by embracing the qualities and virtues of the gospel. What if what the world teaches leads to depression and anxiety and misery? What if what Jesus taught is the only way to happiness? This makes more sense when you think of something having all power in the universe and that our spirits are really connected to him. What if happiness lies in the constant pursuit of holiness, even though this is difficult?

When I embraced the values of the world, it nearly destroyed my beautiful homosexuality and my gentle spirit. The world does not value gayness, but that is the way the Christ created me. In addition to embracing everything society did not value in me, and finding massive happiness there, I learned that I had to be countercultural in order to experience happiness. This can be applied to anyone who is struggling to find happiness. I learned that I just could not believe what society was telling me about myself. It takes a great deal of personal strength to do this and to avoid the temptation to follow the values of society. This is where I will truly learn whether I love Christ.

Am I willing to break from everything I think I know in order to find happiness in Christ? Do I truly believe he loves me enough to teach me everything I need to know about the path to eternal life?—which in the end is all that matters. I must also understand that sometimes the path to love will be uncomfortable. Sometimes the path away from society's values will be difficult, but I must push myself to know it will be worth it in the end. When I go back to my old ways of thinking and acting, I will depart from his love, and block myself off from his infinite power in my consciousness. I must realize that Jesus can be part of my consciousness moment by moment, thought by thought, if I'm willing to deny what is evil. Ultimately I have a choice to love Christ all day long or not, and this choice gets reflected in what I do. I must realize that I can do nothing outside of his power.

I must ask myself how I can experience my own "indwelling Christ." I must ask myself what the characteristics of my own indwelling Christ would be. My suggestion is that the first characteristic would be a love for everything. The second would be a willingness to suffer for goodness. The third would be in adherence to the gospel in all situations, feelings, and thoughts. Through my personal experience I know when I am experiencing my indwelling Christ because it shows me the path to victory, infinite love, and eternal joy. It has a very holy feeling to it, a feeling of intense beauty and radiant love. Ultimately, experience of my own indwelling Christ shows me I never leave his hands. The spirit of Christ is joyfully disciplining me throughout my life to bring me closer to him. He wants to give me eternal life, and a lack of joy in my life means I may not be on that path.

So I must ask myself the fundamental question as to what Christ-centered consciousness really is. Fundamentally I believe it is a consciousness centered in love of all good things, without room for wickedness. Satan will try to alter this, but Christ will ultimately prevail as long as I'm willing to work with him, because nothing can stand up to real love. Ultimately believing in Christ is the way to begin, but it takes loving actions contrary to my selfish nature to overpower Satan. I must accept that I'm here on Earth to do maximum goodness, regardless of anything else, and to follow the commandments of Christ. I must accept that Christ is in ultimate control and influence over my consciousness and that of everybody else's.

Ultimately living in a love consciousness is putting the teachings of Christ ahead of my self-centered feelings and habits. This is something I do on a daily basis. I have to accept that I may not naturally have a tendency to put Christ first in my own consciousness. My sinfulness will try to get in the way. This is once again where hard work comes in. I have to accept that my feelings often will not lead me in the right direction, but my conscience will. I pay close attention to the Holy Spirit's guidance within me. Living in a consciousness of love often means doing the hard work that I don't want to do to maintain my spiritual condition. In many ways it is like maintaining a physical condition by working out every day. I must accept that I need to do good deeds in order to feel good on any given day.

If I pay too much attention to society, I will expect the love consciousness to consist of me walking around feeling aglow all the time. I will have a tendency to overlook the hard work and the self-sacrifice that goes into love consciousness. This is a mistake that I cannot afford to make. Living in love consciousness will often require me to deny myself and take up my cross. Oftentimes it will consist of doing the little daily things that I don't want to do, but I know are the right thing. I truly show Christ that I love him with my actions. I have to accept that sometimes love means the discomfort of doing hard work in the face of attacks by Satan. Satan will always try to attack me when I'm doing hard work for Christ and try to get me to stop. I have to keep a lid on my own sinfulness and work hard.

Love takes a lot of hard work and discipline. I must accept the reality of discipline and work if I'm going to live in love consciousness. It is through my discipline and my hard work that I show Jesus I love him. The question then becomes where does my selfish nature come from? I suggest it comes from Satan. That is why I have to fight it every day. That is why I'm locked in a daily battle against sin. I have to pay attention to how contrary my feelings are to the gospel sometimes, as well as celebrate when they are in line with it. I have to remember that I'm here on earth to live according to the gospel and to make this the centerpiece of my life.

I suggest living in a love consciousness is doing the right thing no matter how I feel about it, and having the discipline to do what is right. While this may sound like drudgery, it paradoxically produces joy. I will be able to feel my joy coming from Christ when I began to live in this way, but I must continue to do the work in order to maintain my connection with it. I must accept that part of love is the exertion to do the right thing all the time, knowing that Satan is always trying to inject negativity into my consciousness. Love is the rejection of sin in thought, word, and deed. If I'm really working hard, I can work to change my attitude about all this, knowing deep down that Christ wants me to be joyful, as I'm working for him. I must accept that I'm here to live a productive life, one that expresses love in as many forms possible. I am truly here to do Christ's work.

Imitation of Christ is truly my antidote for sinful living. By living in a love consciousness, I become a slave for Christ, but in a good way. I must do the maximum amount of his work that I can do on a daily basis. While this does not mean I will never have rest, as rest is essential, it does mean I will do my best every single day. This is a practical way of living. It is something I can apply to my life moment by moment. Living for Christ is truly joyous, and there is joy in the hard work that it entails.

Love is truly action. My actions will determine how much I love Christ. I must be disciplined in doing his work every single day of my life. The joy I will receive is massive compared to what I will put into it. Like most things in life, I will get out when I put into it. There is so much joy in being a servant of Christ, because he is the source of all joy in the universe, and is ultimately in control of my access to joy. He wants me to be joyful, but he also wants me to work hard for it. This hard work is in the daily rejection of sin. The harder that I worked to give up sin, the more joy I will feel in my life.

The expansion of love consciousness will require constant resistance of sin and understanding of the constant attacks of Satan. I constantly need to resist him. Christ's power is always infinite. Satan is finite. One thing I cannot afford to do is to get resentful about the amount of work that it takes to battle Satan on a daily basis. That is exactly what Satan wants. My chances of living in a love consciousness are much better when I humbly take up my cross and serve Christ. I cannot expect to rest on my laurels and achieve union with Christ, as it is a constant process. I cannot depend on yesterday's work to get me through today. I must take the attitude that Christ expects me to do the maximum amount of goodness every day of my life.

I must embrace everything that is in the spirit of Christ to the best of my ability. The first of these things is hope. This is especially the case as if I'm living in spiritual darkness, and ensnared in sin. Often when I am in this state, I will be looking for any way out of it, but may be resistant to the hard way. The hard way is the only way. However, the more difficult path provides so much spiritual light that I will not want to back away from it once I reap the benefits. I have to remember that being resistant to doing things the hard way is a characteristic of Satan, who will try to make me want everything to be easy. The spiritual path of healing is not easy, but it works. If I'm in the darkness that I must have hope the changing my ways can bring me to the light. I must take up my own cross and take personal responsibility for my actions, not expecting God to do everything for me. If I'm suffering that is likely that I'm living contrary to the gospel, because gospel living produces joy. It's essential that I have hope in order to continue to try to change my ways.

Another essential aspect of this process is patience. It will not be easy to tackle sin on a daily basis, and some days I may be more prone to failure than others. I must be diligent and work to reduce sin in my life, and accept that this may not be a comfortable process. I must have patience with God, but push myself very hard at the same time. However, I must realize I will not be able to eliminate all sin in my life in an instant. In my personal experience, it took many months of very hard work to be able to start to feel better and have access to the Holy Spirit on a regular basis. There will be times when I have to go through periods of darkness, and I will not see the light at the end of the tunnel.

What is essential to know is that Satan will fight me the hardest when I am closest to a personal breakthrough in Christ. This is when I have to keep working. I cannot tell you how hard it was when I was close to experiencing a breakthrough in my beautiful gayness, and how much Satan fought me. I must learn to trust my conscience to tell me the truth as to whether I'm doing my best when times are dark. I must remember that hard work will always pay off. It's how hard I work during the times of darkness before I start actively experiencing the light that will prove to Christ how much I love him. He has every right to test me as much as he sees fit as I'm trying to persevere away from sin. However, he is a kindly master.

Another aspect of the love consciousness that is essential is the practice of self-sacrifice in my work for Christ. When I am just starting out in this process, sometimes doing work for Christ will be doing simple little things on a daily basis. This may include being kind to others, or doing a daily task that I may not initially feel like doing. The beauty of this process is that is not too intellectual. Christ will meet me where I am. The reality of self-sacrifice means I must put Christ before my sinful habits. Such sin could be as simple as getting frustrated with other people when I really don't need to, overeating, entertaining lustful thoughts, or other things. There are times I may feel I need to indulge in such sins, but I must remember that these feelings are coming from Satan.

There really is never a good excuse for indulging in sin. As I progress more in the spiritual process, self-sacrifice may mean doing some things that I might feel some resistance to doing. The bottom line is that self-sacrifice will require that I put Christ's will ahead of my sinful ways. This will require constant daily effort. I have to always keep it in my mind that it's Christ's spirit that is enabling me to win in my battle against sin. Satan will want me to think that self-sacrifice is too much to ask, that this denial of self is too difficult. This is a lie. What is not too much to ask is that I persevere every day. It is not too much to ask that I try to be as good of a person as I possibly can be on a daily basis. Because Satan is a loser and a coward, he will try to make me think this is too much to ask. If I agree with him, that will bring his spirit on me, which will feel horrible. In the end I must accept that self-sacrifice is the way to love.

Another critical aspect of love consciousness is the daily willingness to avoid sin and seek God's will in all things. Once again my conscience will have a lot to do with this. Because God is a kindly master, he will not make it impossible to find his will on a daily basis. Sometimes this will be a simple as being kind to others as I'm going through my daily tasks with diligence. Most importantly, it will mean going through my day with the attitude of love for him, and a building distaste for everything is contrary to that love.

Loving work is another essential aspect of a love consciousness. By this I mean loving Christ's work, which can be expressed in any sort of work that I do as long as it is for goodness. My conscience will tell me pretty clearly what the truth is. While there may be some kinds of work that are not in line with Christ's will, I believe most work is good. This is where I may need to pray. Once I determine the amount of work that is good for me with my conscience, I must diligently do that work to its conclusion. While I may face resistance to starting, I will always feel better when that work is complete. This is how the Holy Spirit works. I have to remember that work is always holy, when it is something that is good for me and for others. I must apply this attitude to the jobs I have in front of me on a daily basis in order to bring my full experience of Christ into my work life. Once I've determined that my work is benefiting something good, it is essential that I do it with diligence, knowing that I'm serving Christ in this way. It is essential that I build an attitude of love toward the work that I do, even though the work may not always be fun while I'm doing it. This is serving Christ.

Yet another aspect of a love-centered consciousness is giving over my entire person to Christ, as he gave his entire person over to God The Father. This is where Satan will try to convince me that the Lord is asking too much of me, and where I must be absolutely resistant to his lies. If I really think about it, it makes perfect sense that I should have to give my whole self over to him, as he is my Creator. He has created me to do good works. I must accept that any desires to hold onto any part of myself outside of his will is likely something that's being influenced by Satan. Satan will constantly be trying to convince me that I want to hold on the part of myself and not be adherent to God's will. He will also try to convince me that I don't need to do this on a daily basis. This is a lie. Christ has already instructed me to take up my cross daily and serve him.

It is certainly tempting to hold on to part of my self-will, but the dangers of self-will have already been discussed. I need to remember all the time is that Christ wants me to be happy, but happiness will come on his terms, not mine. It is also essential that I remember that there will be a certain amount of struggle as I try to surrender more of myself to Christ. It is essential to remember that that force which is trying to get me to not surrender is Satan. By surrendering myself in all areas of my life, and leaving nothing outside of Christ's influence, I show Jesus that I love him.

I have to be willing to take an honest look at myself in terms of what areas of my life I might still not be surrendering to Christ. I must trust that he will show me these areas. When I start to see the truth about myself, and my areas of sin, I need to remember that it will take daily effort to correct these, bringing me into line with God's will. This is where I may be tempted to fall short. Satan will tempt me to not put my full effort into sin resistance. I must also accept that it may not be very comfortable to see my sins. While it may be sobering to see, in the end I need to be grateful to the Lord that he has blessed me with the ability to see my sinfulness. It is Satan's will that my sinfulness be hidden from me. This is once again where my conscience comes into play.

If I have an honest commitment to be as free from sin as I possibly can be, then my conscience will tell me what I need to do. If I pay really close attention to my conscience, it will direct me in terms of what I need to change. The temptation will be to rationalize away things that I know I should not be doing. This type of phenomenon is Satan at work. The reason I know this is because I used to do it for years. I would rationalize an action that I knew was not right in my heart. Such type of thinking is exceedingly dangerous if I want to inherit eternal life.

Another thing I need to understand is that having a holy purpose in life will often conflict with my selfish nature. Negotiating such a conflict is essential to living in a love consciousness. There is little room for selfishness in love. I have to accept that sometimes my own interests will not be in line with what God wants for me, which is maximum unselfishness. I must also understand that Christ will give me the power to align myself with his will for my maximum unselfishness if I want this to be the case. This will not always be a comfortable process for me, but it is essential if I want to be happy.

There is no real happiness in selfishness. While selfish action may temporarily make me feel a certain way that I think that I want to feel, it will very quickly retract from my spiritual condition.

Yet another essential for living in a love consciousness is obedience to my conscience. This will especially be the case as I try to form my conscience in Christ. If I'm living in a state of love, then I am obeying my basic sense of right and wrong. I must accept this gift and understand that it is the doorway to eternal life. When I learn to start living the spiritual life, Christ will begin to form my conscience. This is something that I need to deeply obey. The other thing I have to remember is that I need to want it to be formed in the right way. I must remember that a well-formed conscience is literally my connection to God. It is a total gift.

MORE ABOUT LOVE

If I am truly committed to living in a love consciousness, I must realize I can place my full trust in Christ's power moment by moment throughout my day. I can truly be nourished by his spirit within me, which I can feel directing me in feeling and thought. I have to learn to be wary of anything that doesn't feel like love. Now it's time to talk about some of these things. The first thing that I need to be aware of is laziness. This is critical because I will have to exert myself to love Christ all day long. There's nothing that takes more personal exertion than to love consistently. There are so many traps that Satan tries to set along the way to get me to stop loving, and I will encounter these on a daily basis. That is why have to absolutely resist laziness with everything that I have.

Satan will constantly try to make me think I don't want to exert myself to love. I must accept the reality that love is constant work. He will also try to trick me and make me think the Lord is asking too much of me in this exertion. This is where I must go back to remembering that I'm being called to imitate Jesus. Jesus loved his entire life, and I am called to do it all day long. It is another lie to make myself think that I should not have to exert myself to love all day long.

I also need to learn that I will find myself in a bad mood very quickly as soon as I stop trying to love. This I've learned through personal experience. When I get into the habit of trying to love all day long, I will get so used to the wonderful feeling that comes with it that I won't want to stop. It is very critical to remember at this time that I can love simple daily tasks, even though this may not be easy. I can love a person, an activity, something about my life, or anything else that comes to mind. I can love so many things. The critical point in my life was when I saw that I was lacking in outgoing love toward other things and that this needed to be changed. Love can be general and specific at the same time. The thing is that I can easily remember that my number one commitment every day is to love God, and this can be enough to get me through any day. I don't believe there is a limit to how much I can try to love.

Another obstacle I need to negotiate on a daily basis is selfishness. This is perhaps one of the easiest flaws to fall back into. I notice myself being tempted by it on a daily basis. I must remember that I am on this earth to serve other people in whatever ways that I can, and the God will reward me richly for that. When I take on unselfish actions, with actions being the key word there, I will feel myself become full of the Holy Spirit. This is a wonderful feeling, but in order to maintain contact with it I must continue to do things that are unselfish. I cannot go back to my selfish ways and maintain contact with the Holy Spirit. I must imitate this aspect of Christ in order to maintain his presence. Selfishness can manifest itself in a multitude of ways, but essentially it is putting my own desires ahead of the commandments of Christ. This is where self-denial comes in. This is one thing that I have been commanded to do to follow Christ. I must be serious about denying my selfishness on a daily basis. I often had to be tempted with selfishness on a regular basis to learn that following those whims always made me feel worse.

I have to understand that living my life with a holy purpose will often contradict my selfish nature. Holiness is not easy. However, the task becomes a lot easier when I realize that I will not feel good when I engage in selfish actions. The Holy Spirit's presence will leave me if I start to do this. I cannot force the Holy Spirit's presence in my soul. The Holy Spirit is what makes me feel good on a daily basis, and it is a healthy dependence. However, I must engage in good works in order to maintain its presence in my soul. While a selfish action may seem to have temporary gratification, it will ultimately not satisfy me, and will bring me more in touch with the spirit of Satan than anything else. This I clearly don't want.

Yet another obstacle I must negotiate on the spiritual path is resentment. This will block me from love as quickly as anything. There is no place for resentment in a love consciousness. This is truly toxic. When I am in a state of resentment I am completely blocked off from love. I must learn I can react to all the events in my life with love rather than resentment, even when things do not go my way. Resentment is a heavily Satan-influenced state. I must guard against it at all costs. Even when I feel like being resentful about something, I must block myself from doing that. While disappointments are part of life, I can control my reaction to them. I cannot afford to be resentful about anything that happens to me. When I get resentful about something I'm basically saying that God does not have the authority to allow that to happen, which is blasphemy. I must understand that resentment is of Satan every single time I experience it.

Impatience is another obstacle to a love consciousness. After all, love is patient. I must fight impatience with everything that I have. There will be many times over the course of a day that I may be tempted to be impatient with something, and many times that I may have to redirect myself. Patience will be something that comes natural to me the more that I work at it. There are times I need to consider how patient God is with me, given that he still loves me and I have made so many mistakes in my life. God is the ultimate in patience, and it is here that I must realize I am called to imitate Christ. The more I participate in patience, the more I realize there is something incredibly beautiful about it, and I will only experience beauty within myself when I exercise patience.

Yet another obstacle to a love consciousness is an unwillingness to surrender to the gospel and practice the virtues. I must surrender to the full gospel and imitate Christ to the greatest degree I can if I'm going to walk the spiritual walk. I must not reserve any part of myself from surrender to the gospel. This means practicing the virtues to the greatest extent that I possibly can. I cannot say to myself that I will surrender to one part of the gospel and yet resist another. I must take Christ at his word and apply every aspect of the gospel to my life. If this sounds difficult, I must remember that it's not easy to get to heaven, as Christ described it as having a narrow gate. I must accept that I will have to work on certain things in my life consistently day after day in order to pursue holiness. While I need to accept that the path the holiness is difficult, the results will be much better than living in sin. I must accept the constant surrender of my self-will on a daily basis, and accept that this is the way God intended me to live. This is where imitation of Christ comes in again. Christ had to surrender his will to the Father, and so must I. I must remember that I exist to give God what he wants from my life, not vice versa. However, I will receive a great amount of joy when I put him on the throne of my life. I must accept the role that I play in this process as the humble servant, the surrendered heart, and the warrior for Christ.

THE WARRIOR FOR LOVE

I must accept that I am a warrior for love if I'm going to live in a love consciousness. This means I must get ready for battle against sin on a daily basis. If I'm going to take on the attitude of a warrior, I must remember that I will exert myself on a daily basis. I must do this to stay in a love consciousness. I must accept that sin will come at me from many different directions, trying to push me away from Christ by any means possible, and trying to get me to believe lies about everything in my consciousness. I will be attacked by lies in thoughts and feelings, trying to get me to take actions that are contrary to the gospel. Satan will try to get me to believe lies about everything in my consciousness. Here is where I have to accept that the gospel is the only direction in life that I need.

I need to consider what warriors do. I must accept the warrior's fight, and I must take the attitude of a fighter into the ring with sin on a daily basis. I must accept that it will be a serious battle every day against sin in order to win in the spiritual arena, which is the battle for my soul. It is my job to fight the evil in myself and in the world to the greatest degree that I possibly can on a daily basis. I must accept that Satan will never stop fighting me to push me away from Christ until I die and go to heaven, which leaves me as a warrior against sin every day of my life until then. It is very easy to want to rest on my laurels and not accept that I will have to be a warrior on a daily basis, but this is not what Christ is looking for. He is looking for servants who will be warriors for him.

It is a given that Satan will continue to try to attack me on a daily basis as I try to fight him. This may be tiring, but the Holy Spirit will strengthen me in this fight. As I fight I will become full of the Holy Spirit, which will lead me in the process. While this may seem tiring, the consequences of not fighting are much worse. Satan truly is a bully, and if I don't take the attitude of a warrior than I am likely going to lose ground in the spiritual battle. I must accept that it's Christ's will every day for me to fight Satan with everything that I have. I must accept that Christ's will every day is going to keep me happy and that Satan will try to push me away from this every single day. Therefore, I must be a warrior for love. I must sell out in this life to the greatest degree possible to make it to heaven in the next. I must remember that I'll be rewarded according to my deeds, and that means daily adherence to God's will. As a warrior, I must be willing to suffer Satan's attacks, and be willing to suffer, as Christ was willing to suffer for me. I must truly fight to expand love in my consciousness by whatever means I can, and as a warrior I will have to take many actions for the sake of love, some of which will not be comfortable. I must remember that there are no excuses for returning to my sinfulness.

I must accept that Satan will never stop trying to push me away from Christ until I die and enter heaven. That is the mentality I must bring to the table every day. This is not easy. The one thing I need to remember is that living without contact with Christ's spirit is not fun. I must perform good acts in order to maintain this connection. This is what it takes to live in a love consciousness. This is also where it is essential that I break everything down to one day and one act at a time. Satan will try to make me think I cannot do things that are good and that I don't have the strength to walk the Christian walk on a daily basis, fighting sin. This is deceptive thinking.

The only thing that ever truly stops me from doing something is my own unwillingness to do it. Satan cannot control my actions. It helps if I break everything down into a test of basic obedience. I'm either willing to do something or I'm not, and this relates to denying myself too. If I think from the standpoint of whether I'm choosing to be obedient or not, it becomes much clearer whether I can do a task. It becomes a choice. When I look at things this way, the reality of my obedience or disobedience gets exposed, which is good. I can break down tasks into one thing at a time, one act of obedience at a time. This keeps things simple. There are many cases where I will be tempted to rationalize my way out of doing something I know I can do, but I just don't want to. This is where I will be able to feel the consequences of my actions in my spirit if I'm honest with myself.

To rationalize my way out of an action is to effectively lie to myself and to God. This is not good. There are times I will need to say to myself that I'm simply not willing to do something, rather than lie to myself and say I can't do it. When I start to look at things this way, the choice to partake in a good action becomes much easier. It is much easier to get myself to do something when I realize I'm being disobedient to God if I don't do it, and hurting my Lord in the process.

FEELING JESUS'S LOVE

Feeling Jesus's love is the most wonderful aspect of living in a love consciousness. Having access to this wonderful feeling is what keeps me obedient on a daily basis. While I am never without Jesus's love, there are times I feel it more acutely. This takes hard work. This love is what sustains the entire universe. I must adhere to God's will above all things if I'm going to experience more of his love in my consciousness. Fundamentally, the center of living in a love consciousness is putting God above all other things in my life. The first thing I do when I love God is obey him, and this means living by the virtues. Satan will try to convince me that my will is preferable to God's. This is a lie. My active connection to Jesus's love and my experience of it is dependent on me being surrendered to his will. I cannot do my own will and stay connected to his spirit in the way that I want to. Living in a love consciousness means total surrender to God's will. This means negotiating my consciousness on a moment-by-moment basis to seek goodness. I must constantly correct myself if I drift away from love. This is where I need to remember that God will not give up on me if I keep trying to love him above everything else in my life, for that is what he wants.

The experience of feeling Jesus's love the most intimate experience a human being can have. There are no words to describe how beautiful it is. It brings me to tears every time I experience it. I feel it deeply in my soul. If I am a surrendered servant to Jesus, I experience it on a regular basis. I may even get some glimpses of eternal life, which will strengthen me in my efforts to do the right thing on a daily basis. This love trumps everything else in the universe, and there will be nothing that I want to experience more of once I begin the experience. I have to love God on a daily basis in my thoughts, words, and deeds. When I love God with everything I have, I truly feel his love coming back to me in my spirit. He has total command of my spirit. He has command of everything in the universe. This is where I will learn that he truly appreciates my love and that I am in the greatest relationship one can have. I want nothing more than to draw near to him. Once I reach a certain point in the relationship, I realize this love is what sustains me on a daily basis. There is never a point when I am separate from this love, just times I might not be able to feel it because I've fallen into the grips of sin. I feel this love and feel it loving, protecting, and sustaining me. This is a truly amazing realization. This is similar to the realization that Satan is constantly attacking me as well. Needless to say, it is a wonderful experience.

When I apply total obedience to Christ in my life, I feel him helping me in everything I do. There's nothing that will sustain me more than the spirit of Jesus Christ, and it is by his power that I'm writing this book. He has sustained me in this effort every step of the way, and I trust that I'm doing his work in writing this. The more I apply what I learned in the spiritual path, the more I open myself up to daily experiences of Christ's love, which is what he wants for me. He wants nothing more than for me to live in a radiant consciousness of love. However, it is essential that I be obedient to everything he asks. Obedience will help me maintain love consciousness. I realize I am totally dependent on the love of Jesus Christ to sustain me, and perhaps the most wonderful thing will be beginning to direct that love outward toward others in the world. I realize he created me for a very special purpose, and it does not matter what anybody else thinks of my life. What matters is how I appear in the eyes of God.

To conclude, I would like to thank the reader for being open to what I have to say. God loves you, and I thank you for reading some of the most intimate details of my life experience and my walk with Christ. It is my hope that you can digest everything I've said and apply it to your daily life. While I believe that not every walk with God is the same, I essentially believe you can determine through Christ what the details of your walk are. While this may not be easy, I promise you that it will be totally worth it. My hope is that you will apply some of the concepts in this book to your life as quickly as possible. No matter how far down into the darkness you have gone, it is never too late to begin a walk with Christ, as it was not too late for me. Jesus loves you more than you can possibly imagine and wants to share his most intimate mysteries with you. My hope is that this book will help you realize how much you are loved by Christ. There is nothing more beautiful in the universe or in the human consciousness.

John Ryan is the youngest of three children of John and Catharine Ryan, of Pittsburgh, PA. John was born on September 4, 1976. John's two sisters are named Mary Catharine and Maureen. John was raised in Pittsburgh. He attended Sacred Heart and St. Edmund's Academy for grade school. During high school, John attended Central Catholic and Shady Side Academy. John graduated from The University of Notre Dame in 1999.

John is currently a graduate student at Duquesne University. He is seeking a Master's Degree in Clinical Mental Health Counseling. John has the career goal of being a Christian Counselor. He is the loving owner of three cats. John currently has a boyfriend that lives in Washington, DC. John has a great interest in sports, and is a fan of Notre Dame Football, the Pittsburgh Penguins, and the Pittsburgh Steelers.

CPSIA information can be obtained at www.ICGtesting.com
Printed in the USA
LVOW07s0016191213

365768LV00013B/426/P